Encouraging Appropriate Behavior for Children on the Autism Spectrum
Frequently Asked Questions

Shira Richman

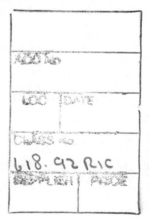

Jessica Kingsley Publishers
London and Philadelphia

First published in 2006
by Jessica Kingsley Publishers
116 Pentonville Road
London N1 9JB, UK
and
400 Market Street, Suite 400
Philadelphia, PA 19106, USA

www.jkp.com

Library of Congress Cataloging in Publication Data
Richman, Shira, 1972-
    Encouraging appropriate behavior for children on the autism spectrum : frequently
asked questions / Shira Richman.
    p. cm.
    ISBN-13: 978-1-84310-825-2 (pbk. : alk. paper)
    ISBN-10: 1-84310-825-9 (pbk. : alk. paper)   1.   Autistic children--Behavior
modification. 2. Autistic children--Family relationships. 3. Parents of autistic children. 4.
Parent and child. I. Title.
    RJ506.A9R534 2006
    618.92'85882--dc22

                                                            2006002043

British Library Cataloguing in Publication Data
A CIP catalogue record for this book is available from the British Library

ISBN-13: 978 1 84310 825 2
ISBN-10: 1 84310 825 9

Printed and bound in Great Britain by
Athenaeum Press, Gateshead, Tyne and Wear

In loving memory of my grandmother, Yetta Verbit,
a role model of independence and calm.

To my mother, Esther Lantz Verbit,
for showing me how to take full advantage
of everything beautiful in this world.
For reminding me, at times, to be patient with my own
children, and for her unconditional, dedicated love.

To my father, Mervin Verbit, for enveloping us
with his relaxed, positive outlook on life,
and for always taking children seriously.

Thank you

Acknowledgements

I want to thank my husband for his help and encouragement in completing this project. I want to thank my siblings (especially my brother and his computer skills) for their advice and for their time spent helping me with this, as well as other projects. I especially want to thank them for the experiences and love that they shower upon my children. I want to thank my son for his patience in waiting for his turn on the computer. He wrote some heart-warming and creative books himself. I would like to thank my daughter for playing "nicely-nicely" while I was working. I am proud of you both.

Contents

Part 2: Encouraging Independence and Teaching Self-help Skills

Part 3: Encouraging Healthy Communication

Part 4: Encouraging Appropriate Activities and Interests

Part 5: Reducing Unwanted and Self-stimulatory Behavior

Part 6: Teaching Social Skills and Encouraging Appropriate Interaction

Part 7: Encouraging Appropriate Behavior and Conduct Outside the Home

Part 8: Conclusion

Part 9: Resources and References

Introduction

Children on the autism spectrum can differ vastly from one another. Nevertheless, the questions that parents of children diagnosed with autism spectrum disorder pose regarding their children's behavior tend to overlap from family to family. Parents seek practical advice that they can apply to specific instances of behavior.

I wrote this book as a practical guide for parents who are looking for answers to the most basic and common behavioral questions. The format that I chose is one of questions and answers. The questions included are actual questions posed by real parents and selected for this book based on the frequency with which I have had to answer the question in my years of work in the field. The questions are organized by topic and responded to with step-by-step behavior plans for increasing appropriateness using the rules of behavioral theory and application. I selected this question and answer format in order to make the book easy to navigate and practical for parents of children on all levels. Although this book was written for the benefit of parents, professionals in the field will find it of interest and be able to read it to consult on behavioral issues that arise with their students and clients.

My hope is that you, as the reader, will come away from this book with practical advice in encouraging specific, appropriate behaviors, as well as the knowledge and tools needed to answer your own additional behavioral questions regarding your child on the autism spectrum, as these questions arise.

Part 1

Behavioral Theory and Application

Behavioral theory asserts that learning is a change of behavior that is both observable and measurable. In order to say that learning took place, this change in behavior must be maintained over time.

Disorders within the autism spectrum affect a diagnosed child in all major areas of his or her functioning. There exists no known cure. Children with autism spectrum disorders, however, can successfully learn appropriate and functional behavior and thrive within society.

This chapter will teach you about behavioral theory and guide you, step-by-step, in applying a multitude of behavioral learning techniques.

1. Maladaptive behaviors: where do they come from?

2. How do I know the cause of a specific behavior? Or what is a functional analysis?

3. How do I know when it is right to try to change my child's behavior?

4. Do time-outs really work?

5. I find that I am constantly struggling with my child (diagnosed with Pervasive Development Disorder Not Otherwise Specified) in time-outs and threatening him with punishments. Although this seems to work, is there another way to keep his behavior under control?

6. My child acts out for attention. How can I stop his behavior when the behavior requires the attention I give it?

7. How can I avoid unwanted behaviors before they spiral out of control and need intervention?

8. How much should I push my child to learn new things and new ways of behaving before I am pushing too hard?

I   Maladaptive behaviors: where do they come from?

Individuals engage in maladaptive behaviors for a variety of reasons:

- Environmental conditions can cause an individual to feel confused, over-stimulated, or uncomfortable. When someone is lacking the communicative skills or the adaptive skills to deal with new situations, discomfort, and lack of familiarity, he or she is likely to express distress in other, less conventional ways. For example, a child may be more likely to engage in self-stimulating behavior in loud classrooms or in homes with more detailed wallpaper and much decoration. A child may also be more likely to have a temper tantrum in new surroundings or when new demands are placed on him or her.

- Many maladaptive behaviors are found to have medical or physiological causes. Children who bang their heads, pull their hair, or hit their ears may have headaches or ear infections. Toothaches can cause clenching, and tantrums have been known at times to correspond directly to stomachaches and digestive difficulty. Even less severe sensitivities can lead to maladaptive behaviors. A child can lash out as a result of hunger, boredom, and/or fatigue.

- Task variables are an important factor to consider when studying the causes of a child's behavior. Are the demands placed on the child beyond his or her capability? Is the child reaping enough rewards for his or her hard work? Is the child allotted enough break time and "down" time during the day? Again, is he or she tired?

- Self-stimulatory behaviors, such as grimacing, hand-regarding, hand-flapping, tapping, body-rocking, body-arching, head-rolling, pacing, eye-gazing, vocalizations, etc., are also labeled repetitive motor mannerisms. These repetitive motor mannerisms provide internal sensory stimulation. The reinforcement that internal sensory stimulation provides is not always apparent from the behavior (a child may engage in hand- and finger-regarding because he or she likes the feeling of moving his or her hands and fingers around in various configurations, or because of the visual stimulation and comfort it provides) and is very hard to compete with externally. Maladaptive behaviors are often self-stimulatory in nature.

- Individuals also often engage in maladaptive behaviors in order to gain attention. For instance, as soon as Molly bangs her head on the wall or bites George, Mommy or the teacher comes running. Sometimes the attention received is positive and reinforcing, such as when Mommy hugs the child and rocks her, repeating soothing words: "My baby, sweet child, don't bang your head." Sometimes, however, even negative attention can be reinforcing and serve to increase the frequency of a child's engaging in maladaptive behavior. Think of the child who bites. Whenever he bites, he gets immediate, undivided attention and the punishment he receives can lead him to act out even more.

- All individuals, at one time or another, engage in behaviors in order to escape and avoid undesirable activities. We all find ourselves watching a ball game instead of doing the laundry. As children, we may have spilled water all over the counter near the sink and on the floor in order to get out of having to do the dishes. Children on the autism spectrum may use maladaptive behaviors more frequently in order to escape an uncomfortable situation or avoid a difficult task.

Sometimes it is very clear which of these causes is serving to maintain a maladaptive behavior. Other times, it is harder to tell. Often, more than one cause is the culprit, as a number of reasons and situations can contribute to a single, unacceptable behavior. Knowing the cause of a behavior and understanding what environmental factors are maintaining that behavior are both crucial points of information when trying to figure out the best way to discourage maladaptive behavior in your child.

2   How do I know the cause of a specific behavior? Or what is a functional analysis?

A functional analysis is a tool used to decipher the cause of a specific behavior by exploring the behavior's antecedent and consequence. In order to conduct a functional analysis, select a behavior that you wish to target and describe that behavior in specific detail. The more specific you can be in your description of the behavior, the more you will learn about that behavior and the easier it will be to work on changing it for the better. For example: "Mark is too aggressive" seems to be a good definition of a behavior that needs attention. "Mark pinches whenever he is placed in a time-out or is asked to wait for something that he wants" is a much more detailed description of the same behavior and provides more information for the parent and teacher to consider when planning an intervention. Some more examples of general statements regarding a child's behavior and how these statements can be defined more specifically are shown below:

General statement	Specifically defined behavior
Sarah does not attend.	Sarah looks away when spoken to.
David tantrums.	David shouts and stomps his feet.
Jenny runs away all the time.	Jenny runs away in the park.
Colin does not sit still.	Colin consistently gets up from his chair after approximately five minutes of work or dinner during which he fidgets with his fingers and swings his legs.

With the last example, for instance, knowing that Colin gets up after five minutes is important information because it guides you to set the timer for six minutes when beginning a program to work on his sitting skills. Knowing that Colin fidgets with his fingers and swings his legs is important information because it teaches you to heavily reinforce Colin for keeping his hands in his lap and his legs still, or to give him a pencil to write with or a fork to use in order to distract his fingers from fidgeting when he is first being required to sit for longer periods of time.

Once you have clearly and specifically defined the behavior that you are interested in targeting, keep a log of it. Include in the log the time of day during which the behavior occurred, the action or event that preceded the behavior, and the consequence (i.e. what exactly followed the behavior).

Time	Antecedent	Behavior	Consequence

In order to help you properly record the behavior and conduct a functional analysis, the chart shown above can be posted around the house, specifically where the behavior is most likely to occur. If the child tantrums at bedtime, post the chart on the wall in the bedroom. If the child tantrums during playtime, post the chart in the family room, etc.

After a week or so, depending on the frequency of the behavior, study the chart, and you should be able to see a pattern forming.

The antecedent, which is defined as anything that occurs immediately before the behavior, will provide insight as to the initial cause of the behavior. By taking proactive measures and trying to change, manipulate, or avoid the antecedent, the behavior may be avoided as well. For example, if the functional analysis chart shows that David shouts and stomps his feet after the lights or the television are turned on or off, family members can try to be sensitive to David's visual sensitivity and limit flickering lights and visual changes in his presence. If the functional analysis chart shows that David shouts and stomps his feet at 12:00 P.M. every day, and at 6:30 P.M. every evening just before mealtimes, he may be hungry. In this case, perhaps mealtimes can be scheduled slightly earlier or David can be given a snack to hold him over until the family is ready to eat.

The consequence, i.e. any activity or event that follows the behavior, will provide insight as to what exactly is maintaining the behavior. Perhaps Colin gets to watch a video whenever he leaves his chair at dinnertime so that his parents and siblings can finish eating their meal. The video helps the family share a nice dinner, but it also serves as a reinforcer, increasing the likelihood that Colin will continue to get out of his seat during family mealtime. Being aware of the consequences for certain behaviors and the effect of those consequences allows one the opportunity to decide how to react. Make sure that your reactions have a long-term positive effect.

3   How do I know when it is right to try to change my child's behavior?

Before deciding to change a particular behavior in your child, remember that all individuals engage in habits that are unpleasant and irritating to others in one way or another. Examples of such habits include nail biting, knuckle cracking, tapping and finger drumming, licking one's lips, and so forth. Not all nervous habits are in fact maladaptive. Furthermore, especially for children who are working hard at learning and changing many of their natural habits, it may be necessary to be somewhat more selective about those habits we choose to target so as not to overload the child with demands. Use the following checklist of questions as a guideline for selecting which behaviors you should target and try to reduce:

- Is the behavior harmful to the individual engaging in it (self-abusive behaviors)?

- Is the behavior harmful to others (aggression)?

- Does the behavior interfere with learning?
- Does the behavior restrict the individual's access to the community?
- Is the behavior age-appropriate?

If the behavior is not age-appropriate but is not harming the child in any other way, you may decide to leave it alone. Keep in mind, however, that allowing your child to behave in ways that are younger than his or her chronological age, such as allowing a teenager to carry around a blankie and/or showing Barney videos to a seven-year-old, can hold the child back in more ways than one.

Most importantly, before deciding to tackle any inappropriate behavior, be sure to rule out any medical or physiological factors that may be contributing to the behavior in question. If a child is banging his head or pulling on his ears, check for hearing sensitivities, rule out ear infections, migraines, and dizziness. For a child who is humming, take him to the doctor to check his ears and his throat. Make sure that oral motor, gross motor, and/or fine motor issues are not the cause of the behavior and, if they are the cause, address the motor skills and infections before using behavioral techniques as treatments.

4   Do time-outs really work?

Time-outs may work to stop a behavior quickly, thus having an immediate effect. They do not, however, serve to teach any new, more appropriate behavior that the child can call upon to replace the behavior that put him in the time-out in the first place.

In order for time-outs to be effective they need to be implemented immediately following the behavior so that the child is able to make the connection between the behavior and the time-out. Young children, as well as children on the autism spectrum, may quickly forget why they were placed in a time-out. In order to correct this, simply state the reason for the time-out as soon as the behavior is observed. Place the child in a time-out immediately using an even tone of voice. If you show signs of being angry, you may actually reinforce the child's behavior by providing wanted negative attention.

Studies have shown that, in order for a time-out to be effective, a child should be placed in the time-out for one minute for each year of life. In other words, a three-year-old should sit for no longer than three minutes, a five-year-old should sit for no longer than five minutes and so forth (within limits, of course). Past that amount of time the child no longer associates the behavior with the punishment and may become more focused on the time-out itself and on when he or she will be allowed to get up, thereby forgetting what he or she did that put him or her in the time-out in the first place. During longer periods of sitting, animosity can build, tantrums can escalate unnecessarily, and the time-out can begin to increase, rather than decrease, the targeted behavior.

Do not use time-outs frequently. Be quick to implement them and quick to end them. Do not become emotional or allow anger and frustration to become a reinforcer and interfere with your consequence. Finally, make sure that time-outs do not become a way of life for your child. They do not serve to teach what the child did wrong or how he or she can react differently and more appropriately.

In order to get your child to stop an undesirable behavior long term, teach him a better way to communicate his needs and wants. If he knows how to react appropriately to the situation that upset him, he will no longer need the time-out in the first place.

5   I find that I am constantly struggling with my child (diagnosed with Pervasive Development Disorder Not Otherwise Specified) in time-outs and threatening him with punishments. Although this seems to work, is there another way to keep his behavior under control?

Make a list of the behaviors that usually cost your child his time-outs. Next to each behavior, write down an alternate behavior that will gain him rewards. For example:

Unwanted behavior	Good behavior
Justin hits his sister.	Justin kisses his sister.
Justin throws a toy.	Justin cleans up a toy.
Justin draws on the wall.	Justin draws a picture on paper.
Justin gets naked.	Justin gets dressed.

Whether or not you feel that your child will be able to understand this explanation fully, tell him that there is no hitting, but that every time he kisses his sister (with a reasonable upper limit of, say, five times a day) he will get a reward. There is no toy-throwing allowed, but every time he puts away a toy (with a reasonable upper limit of, say, ten times a day) he will get a reward. There is no drawing on the walls, but he will be rewarded for drawing pretty pictures on paper (and do not allow him crayons unsupervised). There is no running around the house naked. When he gets dressed by himself, morning and night-time, he will get a reward.

Rewards do not have to be big; they can be symbolic. For advanced children, set up a star chart. Otherwise, offer a small candy or pretzel followed by a hug or high-five. Simply performing the opposite behavior periodically throughout the day will serve as practice and should help to decrease the unwanted behavior with less need for time-outs.

Note, however, that although this program practices the opposite behavior, it does not give an alternate behavior to hitting when one is upset or to throwing a toy when one is frustrated. Additional intervention is necessary in order to teach the child other ways of reacting to these feelings. When your child is about to hit his sibling, if you are there to catch it, prompt him to say "No" and possibly, if necessary, hit a pillow on the couch instead. Or, if you see him about to throw a toy in frustration, teach him to stomp his foot. More appropriate alternate behaviors and communications need to be established before you will be able to eliminate completely the unwanted and unacceptable ones. By teaching other more appropriate behaviors, you will find that your child resorts to inappropriate behavior much less frequently and, again, you will no longer need to struggle together as much with threats and time-outs.

6   My child acts out for attention. How can I stop his behavior when the behavior requires the attention I give it?

Self-injurious and aggressive behaviors may start for physio-logical reasons. They may start because of a lack of ability on the child's part to communicate his or her needs and/or desires. Remember that whatever caused a maladaptive behavior to begin may end up continuing due to the child's ability to gain the immediate attention of a parent, teacher, and/or peer. For example: June bangs her head against the wall and, as a result, her headache is alleviated. Grandma hears June banging her head against the wall and comes running to give June attention. In this case, head-banging, which started because of a medical/physiological reason, has now become solely attention-seeking. Whatever is maintaining the behavior, be it physiology or attention gaining reinforcement, head-banging can result in injury and therefore cannot be ignored. Injurious behavior, either self or outwardly directed, always requires attention even if attention is acting as a positive reinforcer and serving to maintain the precise behavior that you are trying to discourage.

When this type of behavior occurs, stop it and redirect it as quickly and with as little attention as possible. Also, differentially reinforce all other behavior. In other words, get Grandma to come running with attention when June is not banging her head. June does not have to do any other work to get Grandma's attention. All she has to do is not be banging her head. Grandma should run with attention unconditionally, very frequently, and on no set schedule so that June will not learn to predict when to expect Grandma and thus try to manipulate her arrival. Once June learns that Grandma's attention is not a direct result of her head-banging, then unless there are additional factors still contributing to the head-banging, the behavior should stop.

7   How can I avoid unwanted behaviors before they spiral out of control and need intervention?

There are a number of proactive measures that you can take in order to try to avoid an unwanted behavior from occurring before it has even started. Proactive strategies include:

- environmental changes
- changes in routine
- teaching adaptive communication skills
- differential reinforcement of other behavior (DRO).

In each of these proactive measures, the goal is to manipulate or somehow alter the antecedent that signals that the behavior is about to occur. This way, you can begin to reduce a maladaptive behavior by preventing it from occurring in the first place.

Environmental changes may sometimes be enough to prevent unwanted behavior from surfacing. Children who become over-stimulated and act out in crowded, noisy environments may tantrum less when the radio is turned off and family members work on speaking one at a time, increasing the noise level slowly and in increments as the child adjusts. A child who licks red cars and trucks may benefit from owning only vehicles of other colors for awhile. Note that environmental changes are meant to promote positive behavior, but should not be so extreme as to take over one's family life. In addition to living in comfort, children on the autism spectrum need to learn how to adjust somewhat gracefully to less comfortable, more challenging conditions as well. This is especially the case if the challenging conditions are ones that frequently show up in the outside world with which the child will inevitably come into contact.

Changes in routine can often greatly affect the behavior of children on the autism spectrum as well. Children with autism and related disorders may not yet be at the stage of concept formation that allows them to understand that a small change does not necessarily mean complete instability. Try to stick to routines for at least certain parts of the day. Establish a morning routine of waking, bathroom, brushing teeth, dressing, and breakfast. Establish an evening routine that leads to bedtime. This evening routine can include dinner, a bath, a story, saying good night to family and favorite stuffed animals or other toys, and tucking into bed.

After school is also a good time of day to try to stick to a routine. When your child is coming straight home after school, talk to him about his day during snack-time at the table, play one game together, and then set your child up for some independent playtime that may include a timer, familiar tasks, or a picture schedule (for more information on picture schedules, please see Question 46).

When you are not able to go directly home with your child after school, prepare your child for the activities ahead by finding an appropriate way to make the schedule of the afternoon understandable and somewhat more predictable. Draw a map of your destinations. Make a checklist for your child to use at the supermarket. Create a picture schedule for your day around the neighborhood. In a small picture album, place a picture of the bank on the first page, a picture of the library on the second page, and so forth, ending with a special treat. If the day ahead is going to be especially long, stick in extra treats between every few activities or destinations. Work on the concepts of "before" and "after": "Before we go home, we are going to Aunt Sally's." "After we go to Aunt Sally's, we will go home." Ask your child: "What are we doing before we go home?" "Where are we going after we visit Aunt Sally?" and so forth. Try to add a sense of predictability to changes in routine in order to reduce the child's anxiety over such changes when they occur.

Again, some change is inevitable, and it is important that all children learn to adapt to changes and less predictability, as this will occur frequently in anyone's life. When teaching your child to adapt to change, do not expect him to be able to adapt to multiple new situations at once. Rather, select one change or alteration in routine to work on at a time.

Teach your child adaptive communication skills. Provide him with the ability to communicate. If he is not yet able to communicate verbally, teach him to use sign language, to point to desired items and/or to use a communication board. Three-dimensional communication boards can be made by finding small, three-dimensional models of the most important objects /items that the child may need to request and velcroing those objects to a large cardboard sheet. Look for a small toilet at a store that sells dollhouses, play food items, and doll clothing such as sweaters. Practice using the communication board by physically prompting your child, hand over hand, to hand you an item from the communication board. Then, hand him the actual item that corresponds to the three-dimensional toy that he handed you. If the child hands you a toy toilet, take him to the bathroom. If he hands you a small cup, give him a drink.

Picture exchange systems incorporate pictures as a means of communication in the same way that three-dimensional communication boards use miniature items. A popular picture exchange system on the market is Boardmaker, by Mayer-Johnson. This system includes a plethora of pictures that can be downloaded from the computer system to represent almost every item and concept one can imagine.

Make sure that your child's communication board is with him at all times. A child who lacks the ability to communicate his basic needs, such as hunger, thirst, exhaustion, the need for the bathroom, warmth when he is cold, medicine when he is sick, and so forth, will be much more likely to resort to tantrumming, biting and other unwanted behaviors in order to try to get what his body needs.

Finally, make sure to practice constantly differentially reinforcing other, appropriate behaviors in which you find that your child engages (DRO). In order to do so most effectively, see the chart on the next page. This chart defines a behavior in specific and detailed language, then reverses that definition to get behavior-specific, positive reinforcement:

Behavior defined	Behavior-specific reinforcement
X looks away when spoken to.	I like the way you are looking at me.
X shouts out and stamps his feet.	Wow! You are being so quiet.
X runs away in the supermarket.	Nice waiting.
X kicks and pinches.	Good job keeping your hands to yourself.

Reinforce your child for good behavior frequently throughout the day. Be specific in your praise. Be careful selecting your words when you praise your child for his or her good behavior. Never mention the behavior you are trying to reduce or eliminate. Saying, for instance, "Good job not hitting" only reminds the child of the hitting behavior. Instead, say "Good job keeping your hands to yourself."

Using proactive strategies to eliminate unwanted behaviors before they spiral out of control is the least intrusive, most pleasant way of maintaining positive behavior as well as a happy child and a happy parent.

8 How much should I push my child to learn new things and new ways of behaving before I am pushing too hard?

Remember, the single most important thing to keep in mind when struggling with this problem is that you know your child better than anyone else does. Do not ever let anyone take that away from you. However, also keep in mind that, as the parent, you are probably also quicker to get emotionally involved and "give up" for your child when he or she is still capable of learning more. When teaching your child new skills such as toilet-training or when trying to end habits such as a child sleeping in your bed, make an honest decision as to whether or not this is a lesson you are prepared to tackle. If you decide that it will help you and your child, and that the time is right to begin this next stage, then you need to dedicate yourself to this lesson with all of your heart. Do not give up easily, as that is giving up on your child. Be prepared to follow through with your decision and give it your best shot.

If, after a reasonable amount of time and effort on your part and on the part of your child, you can honestly look yourself in the mirror and say, "I tried and neither one of us can physically do this anymore – it is not fair to the child and the family nor is success in sight," then end the lesson. Using the previous example of toilet-training, this means going back to diapers or pull-ups for a couple of months without any mention what-soever of the potty. Or, with the example of a child sleeping in your bed, it means allowing the child to do so for a month or two without a single complaint. Then revisit the lesson with dedication when you are one hundred percent ready to follow through on it.

It is fair to decide not to push your child beyond what you feel he or she is emotionally capable of doing. It is not fair to hold him or her back with mixed messages. This is especially the case with children on the autism spectrum who already have trouble sorting through the rules and ways of the world. Make a decision and trust yourself that you made the right one.

Part 2

Encouraging Independence and Teaching Self-help Skills

Self-help skills are among the most important skills that you can teach your child. A child who is toilet-trained and can feed, wash, and dress himself is a child who has gained independence and dignity. Encouraging such independence in your child at a young age will help him to progress in other areas of life as well. For example: positive sleeping habits will lead to a well-rested child who is more alert and prepared to learn and be productive during the day.

This chapter focuses on encouraging your child to attend to his or her personal hygiene, as well as a variety of other self-help skills that can serve to increase a child's independence.

---

9. How do I find the fine line between helping my developmentally delayed child with daily living skills and holding him back by helping him too much?

10. How do I get my daughter to sleep in her own bed?

11. How can we get our daughter to sleep past 4:00 A.M.?

12. My daughter, who was recently diagnosed with Pervasive Development Disorder, refuses to get dressed in the morning. This refusal is constantly making her late for school. I am tired of fighting with her. What else can I do?

13. My child refuses to get dressed by himself. He is now nine years old, and I no longer feel it

---

appropriate for me to have to dress him when he is capable of doing so. How can I coax him to dress himself in the morning?

14. Which should I work on first: food-selectivity or toilet-training?

15. Is there a way for me to get my child to eat green foods?

16. My son is a fairly good eater, so why does he return home from school every day with his lunch almost untouched?

17. How can I get my six-year-old to use his fork?

18. If my son does not mind, or even notice, when he is wet, how can I toilet-train him?

19. My daughter has been toilet-trained for two years but is still in a pull-up at night. She wakes up wet every day. How do I help her through this last step of toilet-training?

20. My child is fine in underwear all day at school but has an accident every day as soon as he gets home. Why does he do this and how can I stop it?

21. My daughter will happily go to the bathroom when taken but does not request it on her own. I have been taking her to the bathroom four to five times a day, but if I miss taking her just once, she has an accident. How can I get her to use the bathroom without being prompted?

22. My son is toilet-trained, but I always have to remind him to pull his pants up, flush, and wash his hands. How can I get him to be more independent?

23. My son is scared of the shower. How can I get him to wash?

24. My 12-year-old son still needs help in the shower. How can I help him gain more independence?

25. My autistic daughter is at the age when she will soon get her period. How do I teach her about caring for herself?

26. How do I help my son, who has Asperger's syndrome, through puberty?

27. How can I improve my child's gross motor skills?

28. What more can I do at home to help my child work on fine motor skills?

9   How do I find the fine line between helping my developmentally delayed child with daily living skills and holding him back by helping him too much?

Although it is tempting for any parent, let alone for a parent whose child has a developmental disability, to help his or her child rather than watch the child struggle through a task, it is important to allow children to work through difficult lessons and struggle toward success. Children with autism who are allowed to work independently rather than being taught to rely on parental assistance are better able to function both at home and in other community settings.

Make a list of tasks and skills that are not beyond your child's capability. This list may include tasks such as opening doors by turning the handle, climbing stairs, self-dressing, self-feeding, hand-washing, going to sleep alone at bedtime, and more. Cross-check this list with friends or teachers to make sure that your expectations are not only realistic but also age-appropriate. Then allow your child some time to struggle through these tasks using trial and error and learning from mistakes. If the floor gets messy, clean it up. If too much soap gets used, practice again. You may prompt your child through these tasks only as necessary. Be sure to fade the prompt as soon as possible so that your child does not begin to rely too heavily on it thereby impeding his progress and independence.

Try to refrain from jumping in too soon to help and doing things for your child. Instead, allow your child to work through his frustration. Giving your child the opportunity to succeed independently will allow your child a greater feeling of accomplishment and success at the end of the day. Indeed, the earlier independence is demanded of a child, the easier it is for him to learn the necessary skills for daily self-care and management. How much more so for the child on the autism spectrum.

Make time for your child to dress himself in the morning. Allow him to pour his own juice, even if it spills. If your child is able to open a door by himself, do not open it for him. Even if he is having difficulty with a task show him that hard work can pay off, and that he is capable of more than he thought.

Although you do not want to teach your child to give up too quickly, you also want to make sure that you are not setting him up for failure. If your child has not yet acquired some of the skills necessary for completing a specific task, do not sit by and watch him try to accomplish something that is beyond his abilities. If your child is struggling with the pincer grasp, help him do up his buttons. Do not watch a four-year-old get frustrated trying to tie his own shoelaces. Save independence for those skills in which your child can, and will, succeed. This way, you will not hold him back, but you will be sure to increase his level of independence, and you will also be available to him when his need for you is real.

10   How do I get my daughter to sleep in her own bed?

One way to get your daughter to sleep in her own bed is to give her a calendar with a five-day countdown to the night when she will be expected to do so. Each morning, when she wakes up, she must cross off one more day. When all five days are crossed off, you must put your foot down and not allow her to sleep in your room any longer. Tell her that you love her and will give her a kiss in the middle of the night, but that she is a big girl now and you are so proud of her for being brave. Give her a favorite toy, book, blanket, or stuffed animal to sleep with, and let her know that you are preparing a treat for her for breakfast when she wakes up. Children who are less communicative will still benefit from the countdown calendar even if the explanation seems too difficult for them to understand.

If this seems too harsh, another way to get your daughter to sleep in her own bed is to begin by bringing her bed into your room. She can remain in your room as long as she sleeps in her own bed. On the first night, you may sleep in her bed with her. On the second night, she must sleep in her bed by herself, while you sleep in yours, next to each other in the same room. Each night, move her bed a little further from yours, into the hallway, and back into her room.

You can also take an approach that is somewhere in between the two mentioned above. Do not move your daughter's bed. Instead, sleep in her room with her. The first night sleep in her bed. The second night, sleep on a mattress near her bed. The third night, sleep on the floor of her room. The fourth night, lie down in her room for a few minutes, and then tell her that you need the bathroom and will be back in a minute. For this step, make sure that your daughter is so tired when you put her to bed that she will fall asleep within five minutes – a reasonable time for you to be in the bathroom. The following night, tuck her in, and tell her you will be back in a minute. Again, make sure that she is exhausted at bedtime so that she will fall asleep quickly and not have too much awake time waiting for you.

No matter which approach you decide is the best one for you and your daughter, establishing a new bedtime ritual will help your daughter get comfortable with this new bedtime expectation. Perhaps give her a kiss on each cheek and one on her forehead. Perhaps stroke her hair three times. A new routine will provide comfort and a feeling of safety similar to, though more appropriate and less consuming than, sleeping in your bed.

11   How can we get our daughter to sleep past 4:00 A.M.?

Children with autistic spectrum disorders often have difficulty developing what we view as a healthy sleeping pattern. Often, however, children on the autism spectrum require fewer hours of sleep than normally developing children do. If your daughter is going to bed at 7:00 or 8:00 P.M. and sleeping well through the night otherwise, then perhaps she needs only eight hours of sleep. Before attempting to change your daughter's sleeping habits, be clear on whether you are doing so for your child's benefit or for your own. Both reasons are important and valid, but understanding the difference between the two may affect how you approach the situation and what parts of your child's sleeping habits are most important for you to work on.

Ask yourself the following questions:

- Does your child function well during the day?

- Is your child sleepy during school?

- How often and for how long does your child nap?

- Are these naps normal for her age, or is she tired from lack of sleep at night?

- What time does your child go to bed?

- What time do you begin your bedtime routine?

- What time does your child actually fall asleep?

- What time do you go to bed?

- Does your child sleep in her own bed or room, and, if not, where does she sleep?

- Are you tired during the day from lack of sleep?

- Do you feel that this is due to the hours that your child keeps or due to the fact that she is often with you at night, in your bed, or waking up periodically throughout the night?

If your child is actually suffering from lack of sleep, this can affect her performance during the day and impede her progress and learning. Always take your child to the bathroom before she goes to bed. She will sleep better with an empty bladder. In order to get her to sleep longer, you may also want to try feeding her a larger dinner meal or offering a hearty bedtime snack. If you have a picky eater, try feeding her when she wakes up at 4:00 A.M., in her bed, and having her stay there until 6:00 A.M. In order to help her stick to this new routine, buy her an alarm clock.

Set the alarm clock for 6:00 A.M. and teach her that she may only come out of bed for the day if the alarm has gone off. Point out dark and light outside, practicing the concepts of day vs. night. Make sure that when her alarm clock does go off, you get out of bed as well, and do a fun activity together. If she gets out of bed before the alarm has gone off, make sure that all her basic needs have been met (she is not hungry and does not need the bathroom) and then walk her right back to bed.

If you have a child who simply will not stay in bed when you walk her back to it, try starting a bit more slowly. Set the alarm for 4:02 A.M. Spend two minutes making her stay in bed and waiting for the alarm. Once she gets the hang of waiting for two minutes, increase the set time on the alarm to 4:05, then 4:08, 4:11, 4:15, 4:20, etc.

Sometimes you can also play with your child's naptime in order to help readjust her night-time sleeping pattern. With a school schedule and a long bus ride home, however, this may not be so easy.

If your child, on the other hand, is functioning well during the day and does not seem overly tired, she may be getting all of the sleep that she needs, but not allowing enough quiet time for you to get enough rest. If this is the case, ask yourself what aspect of your child's sleeping pattern is most stressful and least conducive to your feeling well-rested. As with all other behaviors, sleeping patterns may be more successfully changed if one aspect of the child's sleeping pattern is addressed at a time. In other words, if you decide to teach your child to sleep in her own bed throughout the night, you will probably find it hard to work on longer or different sleeping hours simultaneously. This is true for toilet-training programs coinciding with sleeping programs as well.

Try putting your child to sleep later than you normally do. If your child goes to bed at 9:00 P.M., pushing her bedtime up to 9:45 P.M., however, is not going to do the trick. Try putting her to bed at 11:00 P.M. Although this sounds like a late bedtime, and it may take her getting used to it, as well, think of the tradeoff of giving up most of your evening vs. getting two more hours of sleep in the morning, and decide whether or not it is worthwhile. Understand, however, that the body takes time to adjust to any new schedule. Trying to keep your child up until 11:00 P.M. may be difficult at first and require your constant attention. It may also mean that for the first week, your child will still wake up at 4:00 A.M. despite the bedtime change, as would occur with jetlag. Eventually, a later bedtime will lead to sleeping later, so if you decide to make this change in your child's bedtime, continue with it long enough for her to adjust.

Although a child's sleeping pattern can be changed, the hours of sleep that each child requires is not necessarily in our hands. For an in-depth guide to sleeping patterns, please consult *Sleep Better! A Guide to Improving Sleep for Children with Special Needs*, by V.M. Durand.

12 My daughter, who was recently diagnosed with Pervasive Development Disorder, refuses to get dressed in the morning. This refusal is constantly making her late for school. I am tired of fighting with her. What else can I do?

Begin by designating an outfit the night before. Depending on your child's personality, you may want to have her select the outfit, choose from three that you have selected, or simply take the outfit that you give her and put it on a special shelf or chair for the next day. Then, start to institute and follow a morning routine. Here are two examples of morning routines that worked for two separate families:

Routine 1

Wake up, wash in bathroom, get dressed, eat breakfast consisting of eggs and cereal with strawberries, put on shoes and coat, get bag, and go to school.

This schedule was written down on a poster for the child to review and follow every morning. Note that strawberries were the child's favorite food so the parent served strawberries during breakfast in order to reward and reinforce the child getting dressed.

Routine 2

Wake up and go color with mommy and sister. Have a timer go off as a signal that coloring time is over. Get dressed, eat breakfast, and go to school.

This child needed some quiet, quality time with his family before he could jump up and start his day. The timer provided a clear switch from playtime to getting dressed. For the instances when the child did not comply, the timer also provided the parent with a clear signal that she should begin to physically guide the child through dressing (instead of feeling that she continually had to remind him to do so).

Other ideas for helping children who do not want to get dressed include:

- reading your child a book while your child gets dressed and racing to see if your child can finish getting dressed before the story is over

- reading a book about getting dressed, such as *Max's New Suit*, by Rosemary Wells

- writing your own book entitled *(Insert Child's name) Gets Dressed* and reading the autobiographical work every morning while dressing.

Finally, if you are still dressing your child, you may want to consider doing so in front of a short video so that your child remains distracted. If necessary, I have also heard of parents who at night dress their children in their clean clothing for the following day instead of in pajamas.

13   My child refuses to get dressed by himself. He is now nine years old, and I no longer feel it appropriate for me to have to dress him when he is capable of doing so. How can I coax him to dress himself in the morning?

The first step that you need to take is to assess whether or not your child really is capable of dressing himself. Then, speak to your child's teachers about beginning a self-dressing program in school. If your child cannot dress himself, his teachers will be able to teach him how to put on his shirt, pants, etc. If he is capable of dressing himself and is not practicing this skill in the morning, having him continue to practice it at school might serve to help improve his cooperation at home.

Again, try selecting his clothing at night before bedtime and laying it out on a chair for him. Show him the outfit and remind him that these are his clothes for tomorrow. In the morning, prepare his favorite breakfast, follow your regular bathroom routine, and lead him to the outfit that you have prepared. Tell him that after he gets dressed, there will be pancakes/waffles/frosted flakes (his favorite meal) for breakfast. Depending on your child, you may want to begin by requiring him to complete only a small part of the morning dressing routine. Perhaps he may only have to pull up his pants or place his arms through the sleeves of his shirt. Once you build a routine, you can expect more and more of the dressing process to be independent.

At bedtime, be sure to repeat the same independent dressing routine that you have set up in the morning. Perhaps you may want to have your child change into his pajamas before dinner or before a favorite activity or game rather than immediately before bedtime. This way changing into pajamas may start to become less aversive.

In this instance, if you need to prompt your child, avoid using a physical prompt. Assuming that your child is capable of dressing himself and simply refuses to do so, physically prompting him is actually the same as giving in to him. A better prompt in this case would, therefore, be a single verbal prompt, such as "get dressed," "hurry up," or "clothing, please," or a visual prompt. A visual prompt is a reminder that your child can see every time he needs to get changed. It is a prompt that does not have to come from you, making it more natural and less repetitive. You can create a visual prompt for self-dressing by posting pictures or a chart of a child getting dressed. Each step/picture should include in it a child putting on one item of clothing. For example: take off pajamas, put on underwear, put on pants, put on shirt, put on socks, put on shoes, tie shoelaces. Walk your child through this schedule every morning and evening, including on the weekends. Repetition will always get better results.

14   Which should I work on first: food-selectivity or toilet-training?

This is a wonderful question because it shows an under-standing of the importance of tackling one of these issues at a time. It is overwhelming for a child to have to change the habits of two bodily functions at once. Doing so would only result in a lack of progress in both areas as well as in an emotional meltdown and possible regression in other self-help skills such as dressing and feeding. It could also result in behavioral outbursts that would then also need to be addressed.

Whether you decide to work first on food selectivity or on toilet-training depends on a number of contributing factors:

- How old is your child?

- How well nourished is your child?

- Which of the two programs are you more prepared to work on and follow through with as necessary?

If your child is past the age of four, toilet-training needs to be a priority. Although it may be a difficult lesson to tackle, this lesson will not get easier with time. It is rare that a child who is not ready for toilet-training by the age of four or five suddenly understands the need for using the potty. This is especially true for children on the autism spectrum, who often never show signs of caring when they have become wet or soiled.

Additionally, the older your child gets, the more difficult and unpleasant it becomes, for you as his parent, for his teachers, and for him, to have to be diapered and changed. Furthermore, once the child is over the age of three and a half, toilet-training actually becomes more difficult emotionally. The sooner you tackle toilet-training your child (assuming that your child is at least two years of age) the sooner you can have the assurance that he has the ability to care for some of his most basic needs independently.

If, however, your child's doctor is concerned about your child's weight, size, or nourishment, perhaps it is food-selectivity that needs to take priority. Toilet-training programs often affect a child's eating habits, and can even lead to self-constipating behaviors that end up limiting a child's appetite. For a child whose appetite is already greatly limited, this may result in unwanted and possibly dangerous weight loss. In this case, be sure to consult with a physician, a gastroenterologist, a nutritionist, a food therapist, a behavior therapist, and any other professional who may be able to help you work on better eating habits for your child. Once your child can begin to gain some weight and establish a healthier eating pattern it will be a better time and more of a priority to start a toilet-training program.

If age and weight are not strong factors in deciding which of the two programs, toilet-training or food-selectivity, should take priority, then consider which program you as the parent are more committed to working on. Which program do you feel is more of a priority? Which program are you prepared to begin and follow through with, even if the process is more difficult and time consuming than you expected? Which program will you have more patience for right now? And, most important, in which of the two programs do you feel that your child is more likely to succeed?

15   Is there a way for me to get my child to eat green foods?

Most children on the autism spectrum present with sensory sensitivities that can affect their eating habits. Food selectivity is often based on texture rather than taste. When food selectivity begins to take the form of color, however, it can involve visual sensitivities and behavioral factors as well.

I am a firm believer that no food should be forced on a child. One never really knows what allergies or subtle sensitivities another individual may have to various foods. With this in mind, it is important to eliminate any behavioral factor in your child's food selection to the best of your ability in order to ensure a healthy and well-balanced diet.

If your child will not even taste any food that is green in color, begin by teaching her to accept green foods on the plates of others at the table. For some children, this can be a difficult task as the foods involved may make them gag. If your child vomits, clean up the mess and bring your child back to the table. Believe it or not, the gagging will stop after just a few meals. If accepting the food on someone else's plate at the table is not an issue for your child, place a small amount of the green food on the corner of your child's plate along with the rest of her dinner. Explain to her that she does not have to eat the food that she does not like. She is simply expected to keep it on her plate.

After a couple of meals, begin to require your child to smell the green food on her plate once during the course of her meal. After a few successful trials of smelling the green food at a couple of meals, she must take a small piece on a fork, and then put it back down. At the next meal, have her bring the green food that is on the fork to her mouth. Remember, she is not yet required to taste it.

One meal later, she must touch the food to her lips. Give her two or three days on this step, as it is a difficult one and she will now have to adjust to the texture of the food on her lips as well as to the color. After she can successfully touch the food to her lips, require her to stick out her tongue and touch the food with it. Again, give her a few days on this step.

The next step in this desensitization program is to have the child place a small bite of the green food in her mouth. The first time she does this, she does not have to swallow the food. However, the second time she should be required to do so.

Desensitize your child to one green food at a time. Do not give up at the beginning of what seems like a difficult program. You will find that, after the first three foods, the program accelerates so quickly that you will not be able to believe what your child is suddenly willing to taste and she will be healthier and more energized as a result.

16   My son is a fairly good eater, so why does he return home from school every day with his lunch almost untouched?

There are a number of reasons that your son may not be eating his lunch at school. Does he need help feeding himself? Does he need help in preparing the food (removing lids, inserting straws)? If so, make sure that the teachers are aware that he needs help. Ask the teachers whether they find that they have enough time during the allotted lunch hour to feed him as much as he is willing to eat. Let the teachers know that you understand and have considered that they may need to help other students in the class. See whether it would be helpful to send some food that he can eat more independently along with the food for which he needs help and/or food that he is working on learning how to eat.

Is your child a fast eater or a slow eater? Perhaps his lunch period does not allot him enough time to finish the food that you send. See whether there is a way to allow him more time to finish his meal.

Perhaps there are too many distractions in the classroom. Is your child better at eating at a quiet secluded table than in a room full of teachers and children? If so, you may want to weigh the benefits of having him moved to a private desk away from the others so that he may complete his meal. Before deciding to do so, understand that keeping him at the crowded lunch table will, in the long run, enable him to become more sociable and learn, step by step, to eat more even when he is in a room full of distractions.

If your child is already highly social (this may apply more to a child diagnosed with Pervasive Development Disorder Not Otherwise Specified), he may actually be noticing that his food differs from those of his friends. Try to find out from the teacher what his classmates are bringing for lunch and whether or not he has a desire to share his food. Ask the teacher whether he or she has any observations about mealtime in school. Social children with Asperger's syndrome may enjoy their classmates' company during lunchtime but may find it hard to remember to actually eat their lunch. In this case, the use of a timer is recommended in order to help teach the child the art of multitasking (please see Question 76).

17   How can I get my six-year-old to use his fork?

There are numerous reasons that a child may not use his utensils during mealtime. He may not have the fine motor skills needed to hold the fork. He may not have the oral motor skills or muscle tone needed to slip the food off the fork with his lips. He may even not have the patience it takes, as food can be eaten faster with one's fingers than by using utensils.

Motor skills, both fine and oral, as well as muscle tone, can and should be assessed by a therapist. Once this assessment is complete, therapy can be used to target the skills and muscles needed for utensil use. Be sure to ask the therapist for exercises you can do at home with your child that may help. Exercises recommended may include coloring with thick crayons, holding a pen, painting, blowing whistles and bubbles, and drinking from a straw.

Ask the therapist if you can purchase special materials that can help your child. Such recommended materials may include twisty straws that require more suction, thick straws that require less suction, forks and spoons that are easier to grasp, utensils with smaller or even larger dips in them for slipping the food off, and utensils made of a variety of materials and textures. All of these items can be purchased easily through special education and speech catalogs, but should be done only with the guidance of a therapist who is trained in the field, knows your child's specific needs and deficits and can explain and guide you and your child through a proper progression of therapy.

Once this is all set in place, be sure to do your part in feeding your child consistent meals and snacks that include a variety of foods and textures. Allow for hunger to develop between meals. This way your child can learn to recognize hunger, and have the motivation to participate in mealtime. Try not to wait until your child is so hungry that he does not have the patience to practice using his fork. Do not expect him to begin by using his fork for the entire meal, but rather expect to see a few bites at a time with the fork followed by a break of eating with the hands, with slow improvement and increased fork use.

Eat with your child and set a good example. Perhaps take turns feeding each other, a sibling, or a doll. Have your child set the table when possible, placing fork, knife, and spoon in their proper place on the table, and remember always to give your child utensils, even when you do not plan on enforcing their use. This will encourage the idea that utensils belong at every meal, and you never know when a child might actually pick one up and use it.

18   If my son does not mind, or even notice, when he is wet, how can I toilet-train him?

Many doctors recommend waiting until a child is ready, i.e. recognizes that he or she has soiled, before pushing him or her toward underwear. The problem that many parents with children on the autism spectrum confront, however, is that this recognition is often not present even at the age of five or older. The question, then, of when and how to intervene becomes slightly more complicated.

There are a number of ways to work on toilet-training with a child who is not yet aware of his body. Take your child to the bathroom and have him sit on the toilet for awhile as often as he will tolerate it. Some children can be taken to the bathroom happily every hour. If this causes too much anxiety, try taking your child four times a day: in the morning, after lunch, at bath-time, and before bedtime. Giving your child a lot to drink throughout the day will increase the likelihood that he will urinate in the toilet. While he is sitting, sing with him. Give him a book. Make the experience long enough to allow him to relax, and pleasant enough for him to want to try again. When he finally does urinate in the toilet, show him how excited you are and celebrate it as you would a touchdown. Sticker charts are very popular but only work to the extent that they motivate your child. If your child is not interested in winning stickers, then the stickers will not serve as a good incentive.

At the expense of having to clean your carpet, see how your child reacts to being naked. Some children who do not mind being wet will still be conscious of not having anything on and will not want to urinate on the floor. If this is the case with your child, keeping him naked for a few days at home may help him go to the toilet. If this is not the case, keeping him naked for a few days will still be helpful in that it will allow you to detect signs that your child is about to urinate. Look for slight bending of the knees, see if he stops moving and looks as though he is concentrating. If so, run him to the bathroom as quickly as you can. If you also take him to the bathroom at less threatening times of the day, i.e. when he does not seem to need the bathroom, you should encounter little resistance. Take him to the bathroom every time you see that he is starting to go. Even if he does not mind being wet, he may learn to recognize that he is urinating and learn that this must occur in the bathroom.

The earlier you can toilet-train your child (assuming that your child is at least two or three years of age), the easier the process will be. This is especially the case with children on the autism spectrum. If, however, the toilet-training process has become too anxiety-ridden, then your child will not be able to relax enough to learn to use the bathroom. In this case, it is best to take a two-month hiatus and begin toilet-training with a fresh start.

Note that it is possible to obtain underwear with alarms and other gadgets to help children recognize when they are wet (see next question).

19 My daughter has been toilet-trained for two years but is still in a pull-up at night. She wakes up wet every day. How do I help her through this last step of toilet-training?

Various companies make alarms and other gadgets that help children recognize when they have wet the bed, supposedly in time for them to get up and go to the bathroom. Their effectiveness is debatable, but may be worth trying.

If a considerable time has passed since your daughter has been toilet-trained, spend a week checking to see if she is really always wet in the morning. If you can find a day or two when she wakes up dry, congratulate her and take that as enough of an incentive to take the next step and get rid of the pull-ups.

Buy a plastic mattress pad. This will make your life easier and less stressful. Try to eliminate feelings of pressure. Make sure she has little to drink past dinner time, and that she uses the bathroom before she goes to bed. Some children will tolerate being awakened to use the bathroom in the middle of the night and then go back to sleep. Try it the first few nights and, if it goes well, make this a routine. If not, take notice of what time your child is having her accidents. Many children, especially girls, will be able to stay dry in their sleep, but urinate as soon as they wake up. If this is the case, take your daughter to the bathroom as soon as she opens her eyes. Wake her a little early and rush her to the bathroom before she normally gets up.

It takes a long time for any child to learn to stay dry at night. Although you will be tired from getting up to change your daughter's sheets, be patient and give her a chance. If a couple of months have gone by (or a couple of weeks have caused her to be very upset) put her back in pull-ups and consult with her pediatrician. Many children wet the bed into their pre-teens, a trend that can often run in families. If your daughter does fall into this category, wetting the bed is something she might simply outgrow. Know that you tried your best without damaging her self-esteem. Otherwise, your efforts will only be counterproductive. If you decide to wait, remember to revisit this issue as soon as your pediatrician and your child's teachers advise you that your daughter is ready.

20   My child is fine in underwear all day at school but has an accident every day as soon as he gets home. Why does he do this and how can I stop it?

Is this the only accident that your child has at home, or is he having accidents at other times as well? If this is the only accident that he is having, perhaps the bus ride is too long and he is having trouble waiting. Ask his teachers to make sure that he goes to the bathroom at the end of the day, just before leaving the building. If this is already being done, find out if there is any way that the bus company can drop your child off earlier along the route. Since your child is consistently holding it in for the entire ride, however, and only having his accident after he gets off the bus, this may not have an effect unless changing the bus route results in a significant difference in his time spent on the bus. Arriving home/standing up has become the stimulus for him not to be able to hold it in any longer, and the question then becomes, how do you get him to wait until he gets to the bathroom?

Start by consistently taking your child to the bathroom as soon as he gets off the bus. Even if he has already had his accident, take him to the bathroom and change him there. Perhaps even have him sit on the toilet, flush, and wash his hands. After a few weeks, this routine may be enough to accustom him to wait the extra minute until he gets to the bathroom.

If your child is of preschool age, it may be worthwhile to consider putting him in a pull-up for the bus ride home. If you decide to do this, be sure to take your child to the bathroom and take his pull-up off as soon as he gets off the bus so that he does not regress in his toilet-training.

Consider that there is also a possibility that your child is more disciplined about toilet-training at school than at home, or is feeling stress during certain parts of his day. For a child who is having accidents at other times of the day, as well as when he gets off the bus, keep a log of the time of each accident. This log will help you figure out if there is a pattern to your child's accidents or if he is just not yet at the stage where he is completely toilet-trained.

21   My daughter will happily go to the bathroom when taken but does not request it on her own. I have been taking her to the bathroom four to five times a day, but if I miss taking her just once, she has an accident. How can I get her to use the bathroom without being prompted?

There are a few possible scenarios that may apply to the child described in this question.

- The child has accustomed herself to need the bathroom at precisely the same times of day rather than learn how to recognize her bodily needs.

- Even if she can recognize her need to use the bathroom, the child described may not have the skills required to communicate this need.

- The child has learned to rely on others taking her to the bathroom and has no need to go on her own.

In order to increase your child's independence with regard to toileting, have her request to go to the bathroom before you take her. This is an important step to include in her routine even if it is you who will be prompting her request. For a verbal child, have her repeat the words "I need to go to the bathroom," or simply "bathroom," and only then physically prompt her as necessary through the rest of the process. For a non-verbal child, set up a communication board out of cardboard with a picture of the toilet velcroed to it. Before each visit to the bathroom, physically prompt the child to hand you the picture of the toilet from the board. Make sure that you never tell or ask the child to hand you the picture, as she may begin to rely on the verbal prompt and, remember, your goal here is to increase independence. This means that it is crucial always to keep the communication board within the child's reach so that she is always able to try to request the bathroom independently at other times of the day.

Take some time to think about when you are prompting your daughter to go to the bathroom. Morning, lunchtime, and night-time before bed are all good times to schedule bathroom visits. This is because waking up, finishing lunch, and putting on pajamas can, in and of themselves, turn into good prompts that automatically remind an individual that it is time to go to the bathroom. However, if you find yourself falling into a pattern in which you are taking your child to the bathroom at, say, 3:00 P.M. and 5:00 P.M., you are consequently regulating your child to need to go at precisely those times as opposed to teaching her to recognize her bodily needs. In this case, begin to vary the times of day that you work on training. Start by taking your daughter 10 to 15 minutes earlier than usual. This will prevent accidents. Then, quickly begin to vary the time you take her to the bathroom by 10 to 20 minutes, making sure to prompt your child to request the bathroom each time, as described above. As the clock time will now vary on a spread of over an hour for bathroom visits, the request along with physical signs should begin to take over as the stimulus that gets your daughter to go to the bathroom.

22   My son is toilet-trained, but I always have to remind him to pull his pants up, flush, and wash his hands. How can I get him to be more independent?

When encouraging independence, the most effective thing you can do as a parent or educator is to make sure that you are using the correct prompt to teach the targeted skill. In the case of toilet-training, the correct prompt to use is a physical one. In other words, one needs to get out of the habit of verbally reminding the child to pull up his pants, flush the toilet, wash his hands, and so forth, and instead physically guide him through each step of the process. This is because verbal prompts are very difficult to fade. Once a child on the autism spectrum gets used to being reminded of all of the steps in a chain of activities such as toileting, he quickly learns to rely on those reminders. Although toileting may be learned, independence is lost.

To physically prompt your child properly through toilet-training, guide his hands through the steps without uttering any verbal reminders. Guide the child's hands in pulling up his pants. Hold the child's hand to physically help him flush the toilet. Use the child's hand to open the water, to take and use the soap, and to turn off the water. You can even physically prompt your son to turn the light on and off. Finally, consider the entire process to be one task, saving any reinforcement, be it verbal, social, or edible, for the very end. (Refrain from nodding and smiling during the process as well.)

Physically prompting a child through toilet-training will better enable you to fade this prompt quickly and effectively. As you physically prompt your child, try to gauge when you begin to meet with less and less resistance. As soon as you find that your child is being led through the steps smoothly, start to loosen your grip and fade your prompt. Do this slowly over the course of a few trips to the bathroom, until you find that you are barely touching your child's hand. Slowly move your touch to his elbow. Then see if at that point he is able to go through the steps by himself. If so, congratulations – leave the bathroom and supervise from the hallway. If not, go back and repeat the physical prompts, fading them even more slowly the second time around.

23   My son is scared of the shower. How can I get him to wash?

You must sponge-bathe your son until you are able to desensitize him to the water. By sponge-bathing him you will ensure that he is clean, pleasant to be around, and healthy. In order to desensitize him to his fear of the water, practice the following:

- Run the water when he is in the room. Do not expect him to get wet.

- Have him step, barefoot, on a wet surface. Gradually increase the water to the level of a shallow puddle.

- Play with toy sail-boats and wind-up swimming toys in a bucket of water. At first, wind up the toys for your son and place them in the water that is in the bucket. After a couple of trials, have him wind up the toys and place them in the water. Race two sail boats against each other.

- Water plants with a watering can. Then add the watering can to your water-playing in the bucket. Finally, take turns watering each other's bare feet.

- Buy a ball that works like a sponge. Take turns filling the ball and squeezing out the water. Then, play catch with the ball.

- Play with all of your new water toys in the tub. Do not expect your son to sit in the tub as of yet.

- Fill the tub with one inch of water. Wade with your son in the tub as you did in the puddle. Then, wearing a bathing suit, sit down with your son in the tub filled with one inch of water. Give your son an ice pop to eat while he sits.

- Water your hands and your son's with the watering can while you sit in the tub. Fill the tub with half an inch of water more than you did the last time.

- Next, take your son's sponge bath to the tub and rinse him off with the watering can. By now, you should remain outside the tub. Tell him that today you want to take a shower.

- Slightly increase the amount of water in the tub. See if this time your son can sponge bathe himself.

- Have your son play in, or at least near, the sprinklers (this should be done with older children as well as younger ones). After a few times playing in or near the sprinklers, lightly turn on the shower while your son is in the tub and show him how it is like the sprinklers and like the watering can.

- Gradually get your son to touch the shower water and play in it.

Very soon after this last step, your son should be showering without a problem.

24   My 12-year-old son still needs help in the shower. How can I help him gain more independence?

Create a picture schedule. Include in it pictures of the following actions:

- a boy washing his hair

- a boy washing his face

- a boy washing his ears

- a boy washing his arms

- a boy washing his legs and feet

- a boy washing his trunk – viewed from the front

- a boy washing his trunk – viewed from the back.

(Pictures of actions can be found in the program Boardmaker, by Mayer-Johnson.)

Laminate this picture schedule and stick it to the wall of your bath or shower. The first few times your son uses this picture prompt, you will still have to be there with him, physically prompting him along the way. Remember that verbal prompts hinder independence. Refrain from telling your son how to wash and rinse himself off. Instead, take his finger and help him point to the first picture in the schedule. Then physically prompt him, hand over hand, to complete the task in that picture. Without saying a word, prompt him to first point to and then complete the second pictured task, and so forth, until the shower is complete. Physically prompt him, hand over hand, to shut the water, take a towel, and step out of the shower or bath. Only then may, and should, you shower him with verbal congratulations for a job well done.

As soon as you see that your son is becoming more independent, slowly fade your physical prompts. The picture schedule can always remain attached to the wall – it does not get in the way of your child's independence and serves as a continuous reminder.

25   My autistic daughter is at the age when she will soon get her period. How do I teach her about caring for herself?

The average age that girls start menstruating is around 12 or 13, but some girls may start as young as nine. It is therefore a good idea to start preparing your daughter for this event at a young age, so that when she does begin to get her period, she is prepared rather than alarmed.

Tell your daughter that growing into womanhood is exciting and that there are many changes that her body will go through and many new feelings that she will experience. Teaching her good hygiene and healthy washing habits will set the tone and get her in the habit of caring for herself properly. Talk to her about blood. Discuss the color of blood and that it is not for touching. Some parents choose to put some food coloring in their daughter's underwear to show what the blood might look like, though this step may not be necessary.

Make sure that your daughter understands that all women get their period and wear pads. If your daughter has sisters or close female cousins, try to get them involved. Have your daughter practice wearing a pad and changing it regularly. Modeling and pictures for visualization will help your daughter internalize this concept. As children on the autism spectrum often learn better visually, mark the pad and the child's underwear with a different color in order to show where the pad should be placed. It may also be helpful to make a visual schedule of how often and when the pad should be changed. If your daughter can read, write a daily schedule that includes changing the pads in the morning, before art class, at lunchtime or after recess, before leaving school, upon returning home or when your daughter washes up for dinner, and before bedtime. If your daughter cannot read, then create a schedule using pictures or photographs.

Prepare your daughter for the event of cramps. Let her know that the feeling will go away at the end of her period and that she may ask an adult for some Motrin or Tylenol to ease her discomfort. Make sure that she understands the importance of drinking plenty of water and that she knows to rest when she needs to.

Finally, plan a celebration for the first time she gets her period. Invite the women in the family and even some girlfriends of her own age. Planning such a celebration with mothers and peers from your daughter's school will provide the girls with a social peer group that will be useful in creating a social circle for practicing, supporting, and reinforcing newly learned social behavior relating to puberty.

26   How do I help my son, who has Asperger's syndrome, through puberty?

Puberty is a difficult time for any child maturing into adulthood. It is that much more challenging for a child on the autism spectrum, who already finds sorting through social cues and rules difficult and confusing.

Since children with Asperger's syndrome, as well as those with autism, tend to learn best through schedules and visual cues, use these tools to teach them about their changing bodies as well. Take books out of the library (*Taking Care of Myself: A Hygiene, Puberty and Personal Curriculum For Young People with Autism*, by M. Wrobel is highly recommended). Use sequential photos, anatomically correct dolls, and appropriate modeling when necessary. Provide your child with a simple and clear glossary of relevant words, such as the correct terms for the sexual zones of the body, erection, ejaculation, sex, puberty, deodorant, bra, menstruation, etc. It is important to remember that although you want to focus on a boy's issues if you have a son and on a girl's issues if you have a daughter, you also want to make sure that you cover the changes of the body that both sexes are going through in order to provide your child with a complete sex education. Autism spectrum disorder has nothing to do with the sexual health and maturity of an individual, and any information and learning on this topic should be provided by the parent and/or school so that the child can learn what is and is not appropriate personal and sexual conduct before urges and social situations may arise.

Topics that you should cover with your child include growth and development, hygiene, modesty, sex, menstruation, masturbation, privacy, strangers, and personal safety. Unfortunately, children with developmental disabilities are at a much greater risk for sexual abuse and molestation. Giving your child a clear understanding of his body and of what is private will help him avoid any possible dangerous or even uncomfortable situations that may arise.

It may be a good idea to get parents of other individuals with Asperger's syndrome together to create a sex education program so that your child on the autism spectrum can learn these lessons, as do most pre-teens, with their peers. When creating a curriculum for such a program, remember that your goals should be not only to provide important and relevant information on puberty, but also to reduce fear and confusion, instill personal safety, and promote independence.

When it comes to their changing bodies, most children on the autism spectrum do not have any idea what is happening to them. Talk about hair growth and the odors of various parts of the body. Give a hands-on lesson on using deodorant, washing, and shaving (the face for boys, legs and underarms for girls). Read a personalized story about touching rules. Provide appropriate times and places for masturbation. Teach your child when being naked is appropriate, how to put on and take off a bra, and how to deal with cramps and sexual urges.

Lack of coping skills can lead to an increase in aggression among teenage and adult individuals with developmental disabilities. If your child is showing signs of increased aggression or is touching himself inappropriately, do not overreact. Lack of knowledge regarding what is considered appropriate behavior and a loss of coping skills when faced with a changing range of feelings is by no means a sexual perversion, and an overreaction on your part can send the wrong message to your child. Always make sure that the child does not have a health problem. Often, discomfort or infection can result in touching and behavior outbursts. Try to redirect your child to an appropriate physical activity and provide him with the ability to escape for private time when he is so inclined.

Remember that hugs and kisses and sitting on laps may have been appropriate for a six-year-old but may no longer be appropriate for a 16-year-old. Your child probably does not know this. Teach him the new social rules that apply to older children and adults. Teach your child to shake hands instead, and to high-five his peers. Start teaching appropriate social contact at a very young age, if possible, because children on the autism spectrum have more difficulty understanding and learning new social skills.

Note that autistic individuals may be more prone to begin to have seizures, be it clinical or subclinical, during puberty, that can result in newly surfacing behavior problems or a decrease in learning and academic gains. Being aware of the possibility of seizures will allow you to help your child if sudden changes in his behavior seem drastic and do not abate.

Sex education for children on the autism spectrum is not a one-time deal. As with any other lesson, acquisition is dependant upon repetition. Make sure that your child not only hears the information that you wish to provide, but also gets to practice it until it is mastered and generalized across places and situations. Regularly discuss all issues that your child may confront during puberty and adulthood, listen extra carefully to his questions (be they verbally expressed or otherwise indicated) and make sure that you are the one to provide the answers if you want your values to be the ones espoused.

27   How can I improve my child's gross motor skills?

There are so many things that you can do with your child that are fun and also improve gross motor skills. Play a lot of catch in the park. Run bases, jump rope, walk, climb, and hike; play kickball, dribble a basketball, and shoot hoops (you can adjust the height of the basket if necessary). Go bike riding as a family. Play baseball together and work on your child following through with his swing of the bat, even if he has trouble hitting the ball. Play tennis, roller blade, and go swimming. Sign your child up for swimming lessons. Swimming lessons are good for improving gross motor skills, body awareness, and water safety. Swimming is the best sport for working on all muscles of the body, including the heart, and is my favorite choice of sport for improving gross motor ability and awareness without feeling like therapy and with the fun of a summer experience. If your child is able to join a group class, sign him up for judo or karate. In addition to gross motor skills, he will practice self-control and following instructions.

Take your child to a pond and take turns throwing rocks into the water. Feed the ducks by throwing them bread. In the winter, ice skate and ski. If you are less than athletic and have some work to do around the house, take turns vacuuming. Fold laundry together, especially towels and sheets. Be creative with your child's artwork. Draw or paint on a large oak tag. The bigger the paper, the longer the strokes your child will have to make with his arms. Color together, so that it is more of a fun activity than therapy. First, color with your right hands, then with your left hands. Hang a new oak tag on the wall. A vertical paper will encourage vertical strokes. Use both your right and your left hands this time as well.

The best thing about working on gross motor skills at home is that it can be accomplished in a fun-filled way that includes the entire family and does not single out any one child or feel like work. Take advantage of that to maximize your effort on this gross motor campaign and use your imagination to come up with new and exciting activities to do together and turn into family hobbies.

28   What more can I do at home to help my child work on fine motor skills?

Fine motor skills can also be a lot of fun to work on at home. Stock up on beads, and string necklaces and bracelets together as a family art project. Draw a picture of a car, house, train, clown, etc. and help your child glue Cheerios, Fruit Loops, Kix and other small cereals around the picture's outline. Little Simon Publishing came out with a series of Cheerios books that help to make working on the pincer grasp fun. Draw and paint together. Paint by number. Paint by color. Use all different sizes of paint brushes, markers, and crayons. Bake cookies and place colored chocolate chips on top of them, one by one, before you bake them in the oven. Make this slightly more complicated by putting all of the chips together in a bowl and asking your child to hand you a red chip, a blue chip, and so forth. The less these activities feel like therapy to your child, the more successful they will be. When you ask for a specific colored chip, do so because you need it for your cookie, not because you are practicing colors or fine motor skills.

Play with stickers, and have your child both peel and stick his stickers onto paper by himself. For children who are skilled at game-playing, buy the games Operation and Perfection. Connect Four is a simple game that a child can play by himself and not necessarily follow the rules in order to work on fine motor skills. Practice using child-safe scissors at home. Roll and mold Play-Doh. Teach your child to cut Play-Doh using a plastic fork and knife. Go outside and play with water. Use a spoon to fill small tea cups and bowls. Squirt water guns and spray bottles at each other and on the trees and grass.

Finger paint and draw on the sidewalk with chalk. Play musical instruments together and create a band consisting of piano, recorder, and guitar. Sing songs with hand motions that exercise the fingers, such as "Itsy Bitsy Spider" and "One Little, Two Little, Three Little Indians." Buy your child lacing cards. Build with blocks.

As with gross motor skills, there are many fun and creative ways to incorporate the practice of fine motor skills into your family-time together.

Part 3

Encouraging Healthy Communication

Children diagnosed with autism spectrum disorders face a long list of linguistic obstacles. Inevitably, these obstacles affect the ability to communicate.

It is of the utmost importance for every individual to be able to express his or her needs and desires. All children need to be able to ask for food, access to the bathroom, a toy with which they wish to play, or a few more minutes at the park. Furthermore, children, as well as adults, need to know how to answer when they are called by name, understand simple instructions, and enjoy friendly conversation with peers.

In this chapter, you will learn how to teach your child new language skills and encourage him or her to communicate.

29. What are the precise linguistic obstacles that my child is facing due to his disorder?

30. My son's language is so atypical, how do I know what aspect of language to focus on teaching him first?

31. My son is constantly repeating everything we say. He even repeats things he hears on television. Peers think he is funny, but I worry about this behavior. How can I expand his expressive vocabulary?

32. My daughter has an advanced vocabulary yet is unable to use her words to ask for food when she is hungry. Instead, I have to guess what she wants while she is crying on the kitchen floor. How can I teach her to express her needs in words?

33. My son's tongue is constantly sticking out of his mouth. What can I do to help him remember to keep it in?

34. My child makes himself throw up when he is upset. How can I break this messy, unpleasant, and dangerous habit?

35. Why doesn't my daughter follow with her eyes when I point to something that I wish her to see?

36. How can I teach our son to respond to his name?

37. How can I teach my daughter the proper use of pronouns?

38. My child has wonderful communication skills, but what can we do to increase his eye contact?

39. My son has Asperger's syndrome. He communicates nicely but speaks with few and unusual facial expressions. Can proper facial expressions during conversation be taught?

40. My child's speech has very little intonation, making him difficult to follow. Is there any way to show him how to vary his tone appropriately during conversation?

41. My child has been examined medically, and although nothing has been found to prevent him from talking, to meet him you would think that he is mute. Is there any way to get him to learn how to talk?

42. Is there a way to teach the art of chit-chat?

43. Our daughter speaks clearly when she is addressed, but is there any way that I can teach her to initiate a conversation?

29 What are the precise linguistic obstacles that my child is facing due to his disorder?

Language patterns differ widely among children on the autism spectrum. Children on the autism spectrum tend to acquire language at a slower rate than typically developing children. Rather than using conventional language, such as speech, sign language, or written communication in order to request a desired item, autism-spectrum children often guide adults' hands and manipulate them (the way an adult may use a broomstick to retrieve glasses that fell behind the couch or a ball that got stuck in a tree).

They may acquire nouns quite easily, as nouns are words that map onto concrete objects. Abstract and relational words, however, are much more difficult for them to grasp. For this reason, autism-spectrum children are much more likely to request objects and actions and to utter protests than they are to make exclamatory and/or reactive statements.

Children on the autism spectrum tend to include a narrower range of grammatical structures in their speech. Even as the length of the sentences that they utter increases and includes a variety of ideas and new content, often they will rely on already learned sentence structure.

Additionally, children on the autism spectrum tend to have a difficult time using the language that they learn creatively. They may repeat previously heard words or sentences, using these words or sentences to fit new situations and contexts. Such repetition is called echolalia, and is often carried out in a robotic tone, sometimes appropriately and sometimes not.

Even when children on the autism spectrum do have functional use of words and sentences, they usually lack the ability to use them spontaneously in order to create a meaningful conversation.

30   My son's language is so atypical, how do I know what aspect of language to focus on teaching him first?

Language falls into two categories, receptive and expressive. Receptive language is the art of comprehension. Children need to understand both the meaning of speech and that speech has a communicative function. Expressive language is the ability to make sounds form words that are then used in meaningful sentences in order to communicate.

When teaching your son proper use of language, it is important to focus on both receptive and expressive language simultaneously. Assess your son's current level of speech, and select a maximum of two receptive language skills and a maximum of two expressive language skills to work on from the following lists:

Receptive language skills	Expressive language skills
Pointing/requesting	Appropriate sounds and babble
Eye contact	Oral motor exercises
Responding-to-name	Verbal imitation
Nouns	Requesting
One-step instructions	Nouns and object labels
Two-step instructions	Greetings
Functional instructions	Social questions
	Simple sentences using formulas, such as "I see a ___"
	Reciprocal conversation
	Pronouns
	Scripts

Each of the two lists is presented in a suggested order for teaching.

If your child is not progressing adequately in his expressive language skills then you should introduce a picture exchange system until his expressive language skills are strengthened. (Picture exchange systems incorporate pictures as a means of communication. You prompt your child to hand you a picture of an item or activity that he desires in exchange for the actual item or for access to the activity.)

For information on how to teach each of these language skills, see my book entitled *Raising a Child with Autism: A Guide to Applied Behavior Analysis for Parents.*

31 My son is constantly repeating everything we say. He even repeats things he hears on television. Peers think he is funny, but I worry about this behavior. How can I expand his expressive vocabulary?

Verbal repetition as described above is called echolalia. Echolalia is the imitation of speech, or parroting, that most children go through to some extent in their linguistic development. Children on the autism spectrum may get stuck in an extreme stage of parroting and need help turning echolalia into normal patterns of functional speech.

In trying to reduce your child's echolalia, the important question to ask yourself is whether or not your child is using functional echolalia. In other words, is he simply repeating sentences and routines that he hears at random (non-functional echolalia) or is he repeating already formulated sentences at an appropriate time in conversation in order to express a point and participate in a verbal, social interaction (functional echolalia).

If the answer is non-functional echolalia, then the echolalia may be serving as a verbal self-stimulation. This verbal self-stimulation should be stopped by interrupting your child with a question. By answering the question, your child will have to stop engaging in verbal self-stimulation, as the two cannot be done simultaneously.

If, on the other hand, your child is engaging in functional echolalia, you do not want to discourage attempts at communication. In this case, instead of interrupting your child with a question, practice variations on his uttered sentence. For example, if your child repeats "Fruit salad, yummy, yummy" whenever he sees a piece of fruit, you can take turns telling him to say "Fruit salad is yummy," "I like fruit salad," "I like fruit," "Yummy fruit," "Look at the yummy fruit," "Look at the yummy apples," and so forth. If your child says: "It's o.k. baby, it's o.k.," every time he hears a baby cry, repeat after him and say "It's o.k. baby, don't cry." By doing this, you are taking the phrase that he already knows and adding a new part to it for him to learn. Once he masters these two phrases, try to teach him a third phrase, such as "Baby, don't cry," and then a fourth: "Baby, why are you sad?" and so on. As the phrases that your child is able to appropriately echolate increase, so will his originality. You might even begin to hear him mix the phrases on his own ("Are you sad? It's o.k.," or "Baby, don't cry, don't be sad").

Additionally, use your child's phrases in new situations whenever possible. If your child is crying because his ice-cream fell, say "It's o.k., baby, let's get more." If he falls, say "Baby, don't cry, does it hurt?" When he is about to leave the park, say "Don't be sad, goodbye park, see you soon." This use and expansion of phrases in both similar and new situations gives your child the tools to understand and sort through language in a way that is familiar and easy for him.

Play this variation-on-words game for every phrase you find that your child tends to repeat. With each new variation on the original phrase, you can veer further and further from the phrase, eventually saying a longer sentence and different words completely. It will also help to play this game with additional new phrases that you come up with for different occasions throughout the day. For example, whenever you walk in the door, say "It is so nice to be home." After a day or two, vary your phrase, and walk in the door saying "I am glad to be home," "I like coming home," and "Isn't it nice to come home after a long day at work/school." Eventually, as illustrated before, veer far from the original phrase while still sticking to the original concept. For example, say: "It is nice to walk into air-conditioning. I was so hot outside." Of course, it will take a while for your son to expand spontaneously on the sentences that he is repeating. His repeating sentences appropriately and in context, however, will only serve to strengthen his language and teach him more appropriate usage.

There are many other games that you can play in order to further and develop your son's expressive language skills. When you are driving in the car or taking a long walk outside, play "I See." Take turns calling out things that you see, such as "I see a dog," "I see a car," "I see a tree," "I see a building," "I see a man," and so forth. Once your son becomes skilled at this game, add colors to the sentences, as follows: "I see a black dog," "I see a red car," "I see a brown/green tree," etc. Other adjectives can be introduced as well: "I see a tall, brown building," "I see a young, tall man." Expand these sentences slowly until your son is able to play by stating: "I see a young, tall man wearing glasses and a blue shirt." This game will not only teach your son proper uses of new words and phrases, it will also increase his ability to use spontaneous appropriate language.

In addition to playing "I see," play the same game with the words "I have." Begin with body parts and clothing, as they are closest to you, and then include objects around the house such as food, toys, crayons, etc. You can play the game with the words "I like," "I don't like," I know," and any other variation that you can think of.

Look at pictures together. Look at pictures of your family at the park, on vacation, having dinner, and visiting friends. Take turns coming up with short sentences about the pictures. Then, look at pictures in story books and magazines and do the same.

Draw and color together. After each picture you draw, state what it is that you drew in the picture. Say "I drew a flower," "I drew a house," and "I drew a fish." Try to prompt your son to do the same. Now, add adjectives. Say: "I drew a pretty flower," "I drew a big house," and "I drew a goldfish." For the next step, draw the same items, only tell more about them: "I drew a big house for Grandma and Grandpa to live in." "I drew a pretty flower. It is yellow because it is a daisy." "The goldfish that I drew is swimming in the ocean."

The more creative you can get in teaching and emphasizing language statements and variations through repetition and expansion, the more successful you will be in turning your child's echolalia into a process of learning language.

32   My daughter has an advanced vocabulary yet is unable to use her words to ask for food when she is hungry. Instead, I have to guess what she wants while she is crying on the kitchen floor. How can I teach her to express her needs in words?

Select pictures of your daughter's favorite foods and drinks, along with some pictures of foods that she does not like so much. Tape the pictures that you have collected to the refrigerator. Whenever your child is hungry, physically guide her to the refrigerator and help her to point to a picture of a food that she likes. Be very careful to avoid asking your daughter what she wants as this kind of verbal prompting may decrease your daughter's ability to gain independence. Since your child is verbal, however, you can verbally prompt her to say the name of the food that she is pointing to as well, i.e. to say "banana," or "I want a banana, please." As soon as your daughter points to a food, open the refrigerator or the pantry and give it to her. Once your daughter becomes accustomed to this picture-requesting system, add foods and drinks to her repertoire. Notice that over time, she may begin to request a food without actually pointing to the picture. This means that she no longer needs to rely on the picture and that you may begin to fade the prompt, though it cannot hurt to leave some pictures on the refrigerator, including a variety of food groups.

Over time, your daughter will probably even begin to request foods that she likes to eat and are not included in the list on the refrigerator, such as special snacks and treats. Reinforce her by giving her the food she requests, even if it means that she has a lollipop before dinner. It is a fair price to pay at first for having her learn to ask for food when she is hungry.

33   My son's tongue is constantly sticking out of his mouth. What can I do to help him remember to keep it in?

Before you do anything, consult with both a physician and a speech therapist. Learn about your child's oral motor abilities and find out which exercises may strengthen the muscles needed to keep his tongue in his mouth. Make sure that keeping his tongue in his mouth is something that he is physically able to do – for instance, perhaps his tongue is too large. Once you have gathered all this information and are practicing the exercises given to you by your specialist, stick to the following behavior plan:

1. Whenever you notice your child with his tongue in his mouth, reinforce him heavily with a favorite treat, be it food, a sticker, or access to a favorite small toy (such as a dinosaur or a train) that can be carried around. When you give him the treat, say "You have such nice lips." This compliment does not call attention to his tongue and, as such, will serve as the best reinforcer. If you are a nail-biter yourself, or a dieter, you know from personal experience that calling attention to a bad habit, even if in a compliment such as "Have you stopped biting your nails?" only reminds you that your nails are there to bite. Be careful to say only "You have such nice lips," and your child will not be reminded of his tongue every time he is able to hold his mouth appropriately.

2. When you do see him sticking his tongue out, try to ignore it. The exercises are what will ultimately help him to keep it inside. If you absolutely must address it, do so by diverting his attention to an activity that will force his tongue into his mouth without you actually broaching the topic. For example, ask for a kiss, give him chapstick to apply, or ask to see his teeth. Remember that if you do this too often or if you use the same trick each time, your son will begin to catch on to your true intention and your comments may start to reinforce the exact behavior of tongue thrusting that you are trying to eliminate. Most importantly, remind yourself and anyone else

who may need reminding that these tongue thrusts are a physical condition over which your child does not necessarily have control, the way one may not be able to control the size of one's naturally given nose.

34   My child makes himself throw up when he is upset. How can I break this messy, unpleasant, and dangerous habit?

Children may throw up when they are upset, often due to their inability to communicate their needs; they do so either as a natural instinct or in order to gain attention and get their way. It is, in fact, very easy to fall into a pattern of focusing on the throwing up, be it by scolding the child or by coddling him. The important reaction, however, in this case is to ignore the behavior as best as you can. This does not mean leaving the child to sit in his vomit. Such neglect does not teach a child an appropriate lesson. It does mean cleaning him up as quickly as possible and with as little a reaction and as few facial expressions as possible. You want to be careful not to give him any attention, even negative attention, for throwing up. Negative attention can serve as a reinforcer, as well, especially if it calls attention away from the issue that upset the child in the first place.

Hold your tongue and keep any reaction you may have to yourself, and clean up the child as quickly and as efficiently as you can. As soon as he is clean, go back to what you were doing before, as if the throwing up had not taken place at all. This lack of attention will render the vomiting useless, and with some time, bring an end to this unpleasant habit.

35   Why doesn't my daughter follow with her eyes when I point to something that I wish her to see?

Children on the autism spectrum often have trouble following gestures. Gestures and other non-verbal cues, such as facial expressions and body language, require an awareness and understanding of other people's intentions that is very hard to learn if it is not already instinctively wired into one's thought process.

Gestures include pointing, shrugging, waving, motioning "come here," and more. Other non-verbal cues include facial expressions, such as wide eyes indicating excitement or a clenched mouth indicating anger, and body language, such as folded arms indicating distance or fidgeting indicating impatience and a desire to be somewhere else. For most people, an awareness of other people's intentions is somehow already instinctively wired into the brain. When this awareness is not automatic, it is very difficult to learn. Even highly verbal children on the autism spectrum often have trouble following gestures and understanding non-verbal cues.

With regard to following one's pointing, children on the autism spectrum face an additional obstacle. In order to follow a point, one must make appropriate use of eye contact. Eye contact can be very difficult for autistic children to maintain even when the eye contact involves looking at an object rather than a person.

Begin working with your daughter on pointing during snack-time. Your daughter's favorite snack should be the most motivating reinforcer for her to follow your point. Place the snack on a plate right in front of her, and point to it. Then, allow her to eat it. Over a number of trials, move the snack slowly to the other side of the table. Each time you point to your daughter's snack, it will be further away from her.

In order for this program to be successful, it is important to keep the trials to one per snack-time. If you repeatedly point to the same snack at the same meal, your daughter will have no motivation or reason, for that matter, to follow your point. Nevertheless, the program should progress fairly quickly after the first few days.

Once your daughter can follow as you point to her snack at the other end of the table, you can begin to place snacks in various locations around the room, and point to them. At first, keep the snacks fairly close to you, perhaps even at arm's length. If your daughter is able to follow at every trial, she will learn very quickly to look at more distant things to which you are pointing. If, however, you set up a distance for pointing that is too difficult for her to see, you may find yourself having to regress a few steps before you are able to continue with the program.

Try playing a game similar to the Easter egg hunt. Place small treats around the room, lead your daughter to these treats, and point to disclose their exact location. The treats should be hidden enough so that your daughter cannot see them before you point, yet not so hidden as to hinder her from finding them once you do point to their exact location. As your daughter picks up on this game, increase the difficulty, making the treats harder and harder to spot and your pointing more and more complicated.

At playtime, point to small toys or pieces of a puzzle. This is in fact a very good time to take out those dinosaurs, Barbie doll shoes, or action figures that your child likes to line up in a row. Scatter these toys/pieces around the floor and point to them in the order in which your child likes to line them up. Although lining up toys is not a great pastime, it will help in motivating your daughter and can be used as a teaching tool.

Take your daughter's doll or favorite pillow and let her watch as you put it on her dresser. Point to it, and after she follows your point, give it back to her. The next time, do not allow her to watch you place the item on the shelf. Simply point to the shelf and see if she can follow your point based on what she has learned thus far. It is important slowly to get your daughter to look as you point up high and as you point in a variety of directions.

Do not forget to teach your daughter how to point as well. You can do so by physically molding her fingers into the proper pointing position and guiding her hand toward an object or snack that she desires before you hand it to her.

36   How can I teach our son to respond to his name?

First and foremost, refrain from using your son's name unless you intend to force him to pay attention. Do not state his name throughout conversation or before you address him. Only call his name when you are ready to get in front of him and physically prompt him to look at you.

When you do call your son by name, make sure that you do so in a loud and clear voice. This will get his attention and teach him to distinguish the sound of his name from less relevant utterances. Once this distinction on his part begins to occur, you will want to fade your vocalization of his name to sound less obvious and more like normal speech.

At first, practice calling your child's name when he is both in the same room and facing you. Make sure that he is not distracted. Disengage him from any activity that may make it harder for him to listen to your instruction. Hold a treat of any kind at eye-level as soon as you have called out his name. Once he looks at you, give him the treat. Make sure that you hold different treats each time so that he does not begin to associate a particular snack food with his name. Quickly switch to holding up toys or other items of interest.

After just a few successful trials, call out your son's name without holding anything at eye level. It is most likely that he will still look at you, so hand him a treat as a reward immediately and give him a hug, tickle, pat on the back, high-five, "good job," or any other social reinforcer that he likes. Eventually, this social reinforcer (along with less frequent tangible reinforcers) should be enough to maintain your son's appropriate response to his name.

Now that your son looks up when you call his name, do so frequently. Fade your tone and the volume of your voice so that the sound of the letters in his name are what grab his attention, and reinforce him, sometimes with a smile and sometimes with a much stronger, more potent reinforcer, for every correct response. Also, follow the same steps in calling your son's name:

1. from further across the room when he is facing you

2. from all the way across the room when he is facing you

3. next to him, but when he is facing away from you

4. from across the room when he is facing away from you

5. next to him while he is engaging in an activity

6. from across the room while he is engaged in an activity

7. when he is facing away from you and engaged in an activity

8. from a different room altogether.

After you have successfully completed the first few steps of this program, make sure that you practice it with all family members and friends. Your son should be able to respond to his name no matter who is calling him.

37   How can I teach my daughter the proper use of pronouns?

Children on the autism spectrum often have difficulty using correct pronouns. Since your child hears others addressing her with the pronoun "you," she echolates in her answer and repeats the pronoun "you" instead of using the proper "I" or "me." Follow these steps in order to teach your daughter how to use pronouns correctly:

1. Ask your child to point to "your nose." Then ask her to point to "my nose." Prompt your child hand over hand when necessary to ensure that she responds correctly. Incorporate other body parts, such as tummy, ears, mouth, feet, etc., into this game. Pronouns are easiest to teach using body parts, as body parts are actually a part of the individual. Only once your daughter has mastered pronouns this way should you move on to the next step.

2. Ask your daughter to touch "your shirt." Then ask her to touch "my shirt." Again, use a hand over hand prompt when necessary in order to ensure that she responds correctly. Clothing is the next closest thing connected to an individual after body parts. Incorporate other items of clothing, such as hat, skirt, watch, etc., into this game.

3. Continue this game using possessions, for example: "Touch your book," "Touch my pencil," etc.

4. Only after "your" and "my" have been mastered should you begin to stress "his" vs. "her" and "their" vs. "our."

38   My child has wonderful communication skills, but what can we do to increase his eye contact?

If your child is a good communicator and is able to maintain appropriate social interaction, it is especially important to teach eye contact. Appropriate eye contact can be a factor in social desirability. Eye contact will help your good communicator to maintain social connections and to attain and hold the interest of his peers. The question to ask yourself is how much time you want to spend on eye contact as opposed to other important skills, communication or otherwise, that will help your child progress.

The best way to continue to teach and stress eye contact without overwhelming other lessons is to place your child on a reward schedule for maintaining eye contact throughout the day. First, assess the level of eye contact that your child is currently able to maintain. Keeping that level in mind, try the following:

1. Hold an item of interest at eye level and ask your child if he would like to have that item. The child will probably watch the item (that is level with your eyes) for the duration of the question and the duration of his answer, thus maintaining eye contact. Handing him the item he requested is the reinforcer. Practice this throughout the day. When you hand your child a cookie, hold it at eye level and ask him if he wants it. Do the same as opportunities arise to

hand your child a toy, a napkin, a book, a fork, etc. Use the opportunity to practice eye contact.

2.   Ask your child if he wants the item you are holding, but begin slowly and subtly to move the item further away from eye level every few times you ask the question, until, eventually, the item is no longer in sight. If you see that the child is losing eye contact, bring the item back and this time fade it out of sight even more slowly and gradually.

3.   Add a question or comment, increasing communication during the time that the child is already focusing on the item he wants. For example: "Do you want a snack?" ("Yes"), "Cookies taste good, don't they?" or "Do you want to play with the car?" ("Yes"), "What color is the car?" Now that you have the child focused on the cookie, or the toy car, you are teaching him to maintain eye contact for a little bit longer before you actually hand him the reinforcer. Make sure that your second question or comment is short and only gradually turns into longer conversation ("Do you want the car? Do you want to play with the toy car? What color is it? Can you describe it to me?" "I like red Jeeps. What is your favorite kind of car?" etc.).

Whenever you do find your child looking at you during a conversation, be sure to smile and compliment him. Finally, teach all family members that conversations should start with eye contact, but that it is crucial to avoid the prompting statement "Look at me," as this verbal prompt, like most verbal prompts, is almost impossible to fade.

39 My son has Asperger's syndrome. He communicates nicely but speaks with few and unusual facial expressions. Can proper facial expressions during conversation be taught?

Before your child can incorporate facial expressions into his casual conversations, he will need help practicing all facial expressions and their meanings. Play the following games with him:

1. Take turns making a face and guessing what the person making the face is feeling. Begin with only two or three faces, such as a happy face, a sad face, and an angry face. Practice a lot, and make the game fun and filled with rewards. Once the two of you have become competent at both acting and guessing these facial expressions, include other adults and even children in your game. Add other facial expressions, such as disappointment, fear, hurt, embarrassment, and so forth, only after you have begun to play the game described below.

2. Buy cards that depict emotions. They can be found in almost all special education and/or speech catalogues. Go through the cards (beginning with the first three emotions of happy, sad, and angry that you have already mastered) and name the emotion on the card.

3. Other games can be played with the cards. Turn the cards upside down and take turns flipping a card and naming the emotion. When you get it right, you get to keep the card.

4.   Select a card from a bag. Identify the emotion you selected, and tell a story about why the individual in the picture feels that way.

5.   Spread the cards out on the floor. Take turns choosing your favorite emotion, one you would want to feel, and explain why.

6.   Create an emotions book for your son. Include in this book any emotion you have worked on together, adding emotions to the book whenever possible. The emotions in the book should be represented by picture alone, so that your son is constantly reminded of the facial expression that accompanies the various emotions that his family and friends may be feeling at any given time. Whenever an opportunity arises, such as when someone in the family feels angry, happy, etc., help your child open his book to the picture of that emotion and discuss the situation together. For example: when your son feels frustrated, open to a picture of a frustrated face. Ask your son what makes him feel frustrated and practice making frustrated faces together. Then ask your son what he would rather feel, and what he thinks might help him to feel that way. Turn to the happy page and work on happy.

Now your child should be at a point where he is able to begin to incorporate expressions into his everyday conversations. Make sure that you work on this skill slowly so that your son does not get so frustrated and interrupted that conversing becomes a burden. At the same time, make sure to practice this last step of learning emotions periodically, as it is the one that will serve him best socially. (For practice material, see *Social Stories*, by Carol Gray.)

40 My child's speech has very little intonation, making him difficult to follow. Is there any way to show him how to vary his tone appropriately during conversation?

If your child is able to, sit down together and come up with a list of ten sentences. Otherwise, select ten sentences on your own. They should be short and simple sentences that your child may frequently use in his everyday conversation, for example:

"I am so hungry."

"I love ice cream."

"I don't want to."

"Where are we going?"

"Thomas is the fastest train."

"Dinosaurs have been extinct for millions of years."

"It's time for my bath."

"Daddy is home from work."

"Slam dunk!"

The benefit of practicing such sentences is two-fold. In addition to working on intonation in a more controlled setting using shorter, expressive sentences, you can select sentences and exclamations that are appropriate and that you would like to see your child initiating. Practicing these sentences should increase your child's spontaneous use of them throughout the day as well. Once a day set a few minutes aside to read the sentences together. Whenever you read a sentence, emphasize the proper intonation. Ask your child to repeat the sentence, practicing that same intonation.

Try to use these sentences when they are appropriate during the day. Before you leave the house, ask "Where are we going?" inquisitively. When your husband/wife walks through the door, call out in excitement "Daddy/Mommy is home from work!" and continually state your likes and dislikes with proper inflection of your voice.

After your child begins to show some intonation and use of these sentences, add new exclamations to your list, and continue to practice together whenever you can.

41   My child has been examined medically, and although nothing has been found to prevent him from talking, to meet him you would think that he is mute. Is there any way to get him to learn how to talk?

There is an often successful but not so pleasant way to get your child to begin to make sounds that can later develop into language. Without hurting your child in any way, stick your fingers into the immediate area of his throat so that he will react with a slight gagging sound. This sound is a reflex that will occur automatically if your child is, indeed, not mute and his vocal cords are not damaged in any way. Again, be gentle and be careful not to actually cause your child any discomfort beyond a slight gag.

After repeating this for a few days, the simple act of your fingers or hand approaching his mouth should cause your child to react with a sound. As you move your hand toward your child's mouth and he reacts with that sound, say "AAAAH" loudly and clearly. Practicing this together, you should be able to shape the sound your child is now making to resemble more closely an "Aaaah" sound, and you saying "Aaaah" should begin to replace your finger motion as a stimulus. In other words, after a number of trials, you should be able to simply say "Aaaah," in order to get your child to react with his "Aaaah" sound, and no longer have to motion towards his mouth with your hand. Now you have a sound to work with and can begin to shape it into language.

As this program can be less than pleasant, it is highly recommended that you work with a trained professional before attempting to institute it at home. Contact and consult with your child's speech therapist and Applied Behavior Analysis specialist about getting your child to utter sounds and about shaping these sounds slowly into the beginnings of language. Then watch "Ahhhh" become "Maaaah," "Maaam," "Mom," and eventually even "Mommy."

42   Is there a way to teach the art of chit-chat?

Practice, practice, practice chit-chatting whenever the opportunity presents itself. Write a few chit-chat scripts for a variety of situations that occur every day. Teach these scripts to your child, and act them out whenever you get a chance. Here are a couple of examples of such scripts:

1.   *At the dinner table:*

Mom: How was your day, dear?

Dad: Not bad. Busy day at work. Were you able to pick up my clothes from the cleaners?

Mom: Sorry, no. But I did go to the supermarket.

David: What did you buy?

Mom: Lemons, oranges, spaghetti, and juice boxes.

David: Can I take a juice box to school tomorrow?

Mom: Sure.

David: What flavor juice did you buy?

Mom: Fruit punch.

Dad: I like fruit punch.

David: Hey! I like fruit punch too! Thanks, Mom, cool!

Although this conversation may not be the most interesting conversation in the world, it has some wonderfully educational elements in it. First of all, as long as there are fruit punch juice boxes in the house, it is a conversation that can be repeated easily at almost every dinner until it is learned. Second of all, the juice boxes themselves (assuming that your child likes fruit punch) are reinforcers for remembering to participate in the conversation. (If your child is not a big fan of fruit punch, substitute a different snack food.)

Note that, although the chit-chat flows, there is no sentence that David is given that is prompted by a question. In other words, every contribution that David makes to the conversation is one of spontaneous inclusion, not one where the sentence before it asks him to join in. Mom says she bought juice boxes, so David asks if he can take one to school. That is much more advanced chit-chat, say, than Mom asking David if he wants to take a juice box to school and David responding "Sure." When David asks what flavor juice box Mom bought, again, it is a question that flows in the conversation perfectly, but not one that follows an obvious prompt. The only prompt for David within his parts of this chit-chat script is when Dad states that he likes fruit punch, prompting David to make the same statement. This is a perfect chit-chat prompt. It teaches David to pick up on what someone else states, in this case his father, and to agree or disagree, as is often done during small talk.

2. *When David arrives home from school:*

    Mom: Hello.

    David: Hi Mom, want to know what I did in school today?

    Mom: What did you do in school today?

    David: I played, I worked, and I had cookies for snack.

    Mom: Did you eat your lunch, or just the cookies?

    David: I ate my lunch. What did you do today?

    Mom: I went to work, I did the laundry, and I missed you.

    David: Sarah taught me something cool. Know what it is?

    Mom: What?

    David: Sarah taught me a joke. Why is a giraffe's neck so long?

    Mom: Why?

    David: Because he has smelly feet.

Arrange with Sarah, or a friend/teacher/bus driver in your child's school to teach him something "cool" every day so that a new "cool" thing can be inserted into David's answer every day. Jokes are an advanced concept for children on the autism spectrum. If your child still needs to work on the concept of a joke, do so at a separate time and not while working on the art of chit-chat so as not to confuse your child with too many new things to learn at once. Instead of a joke, have the friend/ teacher/bus driver teach your child a demonstration of a high-five, an interesting fact, or a "cool" drawing.

What is nice about the second conversation is that it is not completely grammatical ("Know what it is?") and it includes slang words ("cool"). When teaching your child how to chit-chat, it is very important to teach him to sound age-appropriate. Clearly, if he is at the stage where he is learning chit-chat and conversation, you will want him to be interesting and fun to talk to within his peer group. Make sure that you are versed in the phrases and activities that your child's peers find "cool" so that your child's chit-chat will serve him well socially.

Remember that the more scripts you practice, the more variation you can teach. Insert pretzels as the snack in your script instead of cookies. Have yourself going for a walk instead of doing the laundry. The more variation of scripts you practice, the more your son will suddenly begin to create his own variations as well. You may be surprised by his spontaneous creativity after what seems like much repetition.

43   Our daughter speaks clearly when she is addressed, but is there any way that I can teach her to initiate a conversation?

The best way to teach your daughter to initiate conversations is constantly to comment on your surroundings and to teach her to do the same. When you walk into a room, comment on what and whom you see. Although it may sound mechanical to repeat the same conversation starter, doing so will allow your daughter to pick up on it and use it, starting her own conversations. Play the games "I see," "I am drawing," and so forth as discussed in the question regarding echolalia (see Question 31).

When you begin a conversation, tell her whom you are going to talk to ("I am going to say hello to Aunt Shirley"). The more specific you can be about the conversation you are about to have, the more it will teach your daughter the art of initiating, i.e. whom to approach and what to talk about in a conversation.

Be careful not to say "Do you want to come talk to Aunt Shirley with me?" or "Let's go say hello to Uncle Bob." These phrases do include your daughter in the conversations, but will not teach her to initiate in the same way. By saying "I am going to…" you constantly place the idea of "I am going to" in her mind so that when she walks into a room full of people, she will think "I am going to talk to someone" and hopefully, eventually, go and do it on her own. Do not ask her whom she is going to talk to either. Remember, you want her to initiate, and you want her to think of initiating. Rather, be careful to say "I am going to ask Suzanne about her new school," "I am going to tell Julia that I like her jacket," or "I am going to ask Grandma how she baked so many cookies."

Another way you can work on initiating is by creating a situation in which your daughter needs something in order to continue with her activity. Sit down at the dinner table without forks, and wait for her to ask for one. Draw together, but forget to get the markers or the paper. If she is reading a book, shut off the light and wait for her to say something. If she says nothing but only gets frustrated, prompt her verbally by saying "Say: 'Mommy, turn on the light, please. I can't read in the dark.'"

Send your daughter to get something from your room that is not in the room. Have your husband or a sibling or friend wait in your room, and see if she initiates a conversation with them asking for help. If she does not do so, model a conversation for her. Wait a day or two and set up the same situation, only this time ask your husband to get something from your room. Remember to ask for something that cannot be found there. Have him take your daughter with him, and when he gets to your room and sees that what you asked for cannot be found, your daughter will observe him asking the friend in your room if she knows where the item is.

Recreate this scenario enough times so that when you are ready to ask your daughter to be in the role of the one who is to fetch you an item from your room, she will automatically ask your friend where it is, thereby initiating a conversation.

Practiced conversations such as the one described above are not spontaneous initiation. Remember, however, that they are a means to a goal, and the more situations that you are able to fabricate and practice, the more practice your daughter will get in initiating and, thus, the more likely she will be to do so on her own.

Part 4

Encouraging Appropriate Activities and Interests

Despite varying levels of cognitive functioning, all children on the autism spectrum exhibit difficulty directing themselves toward appropriate activities. Some children on the autism spectrum enjoy quickly flipping through the pages of books instead of reading them. Some line up objects, such as toy dinosaurs, by size, color, or shape. Some may walk from room to room, carrying toys with them wherever they go, while others opt to remain by their mother's side at all times either staring into space, or running and jumping energetically.

Children on the autism spectrum often show little or no interest in playing with toys. Those who do develop an interest may obsess on that interest to the exclusion of other activities, for example, by spending all of their time playing with and talking about trains.

In this section, you will learn how to gain your child's attention and engage him in appropriate activities while discouraging inappropriate ones. You will also learn how to develop your child's interests while limiting those interests to appropriate places and times.

44. My son always seems very distant. How can I get him more involved?

45. I cannot get my child to sit in a chair. His inability to sit still is affecting him at mealtime, during playtime, and at preschool. Aside from giving him medication, what can I do?

46. How can I encourage my child to show interest in playing?

47. My son spends his free time lining up objects and toys. How can I get him to play more appropriately?

48. My son spins the wheels of his toy cars. How can I encourage him to play with the cars instead?

49. My son has trouble following the rules of games. How can we teach him some simple games he can play with the family?

50. My son systematically takes every book out of our bookcase and flips through each so quickly that I barely manage to read one sentence to him out loud. How can I make reading more educational?

51. The neighbors are complaining about the noise coming from my apartment, but I have two very energetic, autistic sons. What is the best way for me to handle this situation?

52. We have a four-bedroom house with a nice den and playroom, yet my son refuses to leave my side, opting to sit on the kitchen floor if I am cooking or run around the table if I am sitting at it paying bills. I would love for him to make use of the other rooms in the house and play, even if I am not sitting by his side. What should I do?

53. My son goes from room to room gathering up all of his toys and carrying them around the house with him. He needs to take approximately ten of his small belongings with him wherever we go. How can I convince him to leave some of his things behind?

54. My son is only interested in trains. How can I get him to play with any other toy or talk about any other subject?

44   My son always seems very distant. How can I get him more involved?

The more you interact with your son, the more involved he will be. Talk to your son all day long whether he answers you or not. Tell him everything that you are doing as you do it throughout the day whether he seems to understand you or not. If he is not paying attention, work on getting his attention. You can do this most easily by playing games that have a cause and an effect. For example:

- Play peek-a-boo with your son. Sit close to him and use a towel to hide your face, as it is a more tangible prop than your hands are. Select a brightly colored towel in order to grab his attention, and pull it down, calling "Peek-a-boo!" with as much animation in your body, expressions, and voice as you can muster. If he still does not respond, tickle him after each trial.

- Take a doll or teddy bear and walk it up his leg, saying, "I'm going to get you," building anticipation in your voice. When you reach his face, shake the doll or the teddy bear as if it is kissing him and cheer. Eventually, build up to starting the anticipation from as far away as across the room.

- Play "I am going to get you" in other non-scary situations such as crawling across the floor.

- Give your son a ball. As soon as he throws or even drops the ball, cheer him on, pick up the ball, and give it back to him.

- Build a tower of blocks and prompt him to knock them down. Cheer the demolition together. If your son is capable of building towers, take turns being the construction and the demolition crew.

- Splash the water in your son's bath together. Time your splashes so that they are coordinated with your son's. Begin by following his lead in splashing and stopping. Then see if he is ready to follow your lead.

- Play musical band. Get out some maracas and a couple of drums. Shake the maracas at the same time, again beginning the game by following your son's lead. Then bang your maraca on a drum. If he does not follow your lead, physically prompt him to do so. Make sure that you coordinate your music-making so that you are either both shaking the maracas or both banging them.

Even older children can play these games in order to establish interaction. Note that a jack-in-the-box is a toy that works on the concept of cause and effect, and yet I did not recommend it in this section. This is because the cause and effect that is desired is one that involves another human being and teaches the child about interaction, learning by imitation, and showing interest in the activity around him.

45   I cannot get my child to sit in a chair. His inability to sit still is affecting him at mealtime, during playtime, and at preschool. Aside from giving him medication, what can I do?

Start very slowly by holding your child in the chair until he looks at you or, if he tantrums, until he stops. The moment either of those occur (even for the span of a breath), let him up. Repeat this throughout the day for a few days. Initial resistance to sitting should subside as your child learns that he is not expected to stay sitting for too long.

Once your child's initial resistance to sitting is gone, you can now expect him to sit for two or three seconds. During this time, count, clap, etc. so that you keep his attention, and then let him get up. Again, practice this periodically throughout the day. Now you are ready to work on ten seconds. Try singing a longer song and letting your child up at the song's completion.

Increase sitting time to 30 seconds, a minute, three minutes, five minutes, ten, etc. During sitting time be sure to engage your child in an activity such as reading a book, sorting, coloring, and eating. Change the activity from trial to trial. Changing activities will make sitting less boring and your child will learn to generalize this skill throughout different situations. As the time that your child is required to sit increases it would be wise to introduce a timer. When the buzzer goes off, prompt him to get up right away and have free time as a break.

This method is only effective if you, as a parent, have the patience to repeat each small step over and over and make the steps small enough so that over 65 percent of the time your child is successful. Only move on to the next step when your child is successful 80 percent of the time or more.

46   How can I encourage my child to show interest in playing?

When selecting toys and materials for your child, keep in mind his individual skills and capabilities. It may be necessary to modify the rules of a game to meet his level, or buy special materials (such as large grip crayons, puzzles with knobs, and so forth) to match his motor skills.

Create a play area for your child. Block off the area to reduce distractions and set it up in an area of the house toward which he already tends to gravitate.

Teach your child how to manipulate simple toys, such as pop-up toys, tops, shape sorters, puzzles, and peg boards, by prompting him hand over hand and slowly fading the prompt and allowing him more independence with the toy as you see that he is able. Once your child can manipulate simple toys, place these toys in his play area and physically lead him from one to another until a routine is established.

Children who are already skilled at certain toys and games should have those toys and games accessible to them at all times. In order to ensure, however, that your child does not get bored with the selection, rotate the toys, keeping some in the closet and some within your child's reach, switching them around periodically.

Work with your child on playing independently for short periods of time. Set up a timer for three minutes, reinforcing him for playing nicely when the timer goes off. Slowly increase the number of minutes during which you expect him to play. A timer can also be used to signal that it is time to switch to a new toy.

Create a picture schedule for your child to follow during play time. To do so, place a picture of an activity that he is able to complete independently in the front page of a picture album. On the next page, place a picture of a treat, such as a candy or a pretzel, that can serve as a positive reinforcer. Physically prompt your child to open the album, point to the first page, and retrieve the toy in the picture. After he has finished playing, physically prompt him to put the toy away, return to the album, turn the page, point to the next picture, and get his treat. Be careful to physically guide him through the task without giving him any verbal cues, as he may quickly learn to rely on verbal cues and our goal is to increase his independence in playing. Practice this picture schedule every day, slowly adding pictures and games at random throughout the album.

Remember periodically to add reinforcers and treats throughout the album as well, especially when he is expected to play with more toys and for longer periods of time.

Model appropriate play frequently. Take a car and run it across the floor saying "vroom, vroom." Set up frequent tea parties. Play dress up, house, and store together as a family. Take a video of you and other family members playing these and other games. When your child watches the video, have the appropriate materials available so that he can imitate what he sees on screen, and eventually create variations of the play scenario he has learned.

Playing is more than just fun. It is an important part of a child's development and should be constantly emphasized as a tool for learning.

47   My son spends his free time lining up objects and toys. How can I get him to play more appropriately?

Lining up objects and toys is a natural step in the progression of playing that all children go through as they develop. The question then becomes, at what point is lining objects too extreme and how do we monitor it so that it does not occur to the exclusion of other play activities?

1. When teaching appropriate play to your child, avoid having the expectation that the lining up of toys will be eliminated from the child's repertoire completely. Rather, try to make the habit more appropriate.

2. Lining up books or spoons is not considered an appropriate form of play. However, lining up race cars before a race begins is appropriate.

3.   Any of the following steps can be used to teach appropriate lining of toys:

- Allow your child to line up race cars. At the completion of this task, physically prompt him, hand over hand, to race the cars across the floor.

- Teach your child to line up tea cups and dolls. Physically prompt her to then pour tea for a tea party.

- Help your child line up blocks by color and shape. Start with a bottom row, and build up. Work on varying the lineup, one block at a time, so that the color and shape pattern of the block tower can begin to change.

You can also decrease the amount of time that your child engages in lining up objects by setting a timer for one to five minutes, depending on your child, and model/expect appropriate play for that amount of time. When the timer goes off, allow the child free time during which the lining of objects takes place. Slowly increase the amount of time you expect the child to engage in appropriate play while decreasing the amount of time you allow for "free-play."

48   My son spins the wheels of his toy cars. How can I encourage him to play with the cars instead?

Model pretend driving of the toy car across the floor, along with the sound "vroom, vroom." Take your child's hand, and physically prompt him to do the same. Teach him this repeatedly and throughout the day, heavily reinforcing him and praising him. Try to make this game as much fun as possible by using giggles, tickles, music, and candy.

Next, see if your son can pick up on the game without the hand over hand prompt. Take a car and model appropriate playing. Hand him the car and say "your turn" and see if he can do the same.

As briefly mentioned in Question 46, video modeling has been proven to be a very effective method for teaching pretend play. Film yourself playing appropriately with toy cars for five minutes. Make sure that there are no distractions in the background of the video. Play in an area that is clean and free of clutter, preferably in your child's playroom. Use your voice to create vehicle sound effects that your child can learn to imitate. Drive the car around the room. Make a few cars race against each other, saying "One, two, three, and they're off! It looks like the red car is going to win... but no! The blue car is the winner. Hurray for the blue car!" Use all of your imagination and, if you are able, watch other children playing with cars to help develop your own ideas and film more realistic, age-appropriate scenarios. Show this video to your child before he plays. After a couple of viewings, make the toy cars available to him while the video is on. If need be, you can play with the cars, either mimicking the video live or prompting him hand over hand while he watches the film.

If you find that you are having trouble getting your child to imitate and play along while watching the video, backtrack by creating a video of you playing Simon Says, and watch it with your child. Simon Says is an interactive game that is easy to physically prompt from behind and can serve as a model for imitating play scenarios on video. To play Simon Says, issue a one-step command prefacing it with the words "Simon Says." For example: "Simon Says touch your nose." Touching the incorrect body part can be used as a criterion for being "out" before children are ready to distinguish between when Simon gave the command and when "Simon did not say so."

Most children, including children on the autism spectrum, enjoy imitating songs and scenarios that they see on television. Use this to your advantage and create a variety of pretend play videos. It will not only help your child to learn valuable play skills, it will also free you from having to be the active teacher and allow you some free time during which your child is engaging in appropriate play and learning. Some ideas for other games to film include: tea party, doll house, farm animals, and dinosaurs.

Finally, if your child knows how to play with the car and yet is reluctant to do so, try setting a timer for a few minutes during which your child must play appropriately. When the buzzer sounds, allow your child a one minute break during which he can play as he pleases. Then, reset the timer. The break is the only reinforcer that you will need. If your child forgets to play appropriately while the timer is still going, remind him and reset the timer. Slowly increase the time during which appropriate playing is expected.

49   My son has trouble following the rules of games. How can we teach him some simple games he can play with the family?

This is a wonderful question and an important goal, as it will serve to include the child in the family's social dynamic, improving sibling relationships while teaching him valuable skills at the same time. Before trying to include your son in the family game-playing already established, it may be a good idea to first establish some new family games around him. This may make it easier for him to begin to participate and play together with others and also help the siblings to begin to play with him without feeling that their games are compromised.

Depending on your child's current play repertoire, try to teach him to follow Simon Says. Siblings of any age will be willing to participate if they are allowed to be Simon. Memory can be played with fewer cards as a simple turn-taking and matching game, as can Barnyard Bingo and Lucky Ducks. When introducing these games to your child, take two weeks to practice and play with him yourself, or have him practice with another adult, before you have him join other children in the family. Giving him a greater familiarity with the game first will allow the family game-playing to run more smoothly.

Once these games become somewhat routine, start to look at the games that your children play together and see if there are any aspects of them that can be taught to your child who is on the autism spectrum. For example, if you are playing Monopoly, you may be able to make your child with autism the dice roller or the piece mover. For Battleship, you can try to give him a board and teach him to put a peg in a random slot on a ship every time a number is called, even if the number does not match up with that battleship.

You will be surprised at the amount of patience and rule-bending the siblings will allow in order to include others as long as it is done fairly and consistently, and explained to them as though they are the mature ones having a hand in the teaching. It would be nice, in fact, to then include the children in a game of Scrabble that you and other adults could play, this time bending the rules for the siblings and allowing, say, all spellings, correct or incorrect, to count for those under the age of 11.

50   My son systematically takes every book out of our bookcase and flips through each so quickly that I barely manage to read one sentence to him out loud. How can I make reading more educational?

Start with one short book that has a familiar storyline or is written to a familiar song. Pull your child aside and periodically read the first two pages of this book to him while focusing him on looking at the book and turning one page. After you have completed reading the second page (each page should have no more than one or two short sentences, or even just a few words, depending on the child's attention span) reinforce him with a small snack or candy that he likes to eat. At the same time, whenever you see your child approaching the bookcase physically prompt him to select the book you are working on reading together. Read the same two pages together. Then allow him to continue flipping through the books as he has been doing. Slowly he will learn to read the two pages you selected before he flips through the rest of the books, as the flipping itself is a reinforcer. Once he is proficiently slowing down for those two pages, add a third page, and so forth, until he is able to read one book, page by page, before beginning his flipping routine.

I would be strict about physically prompting him to return a book that he has flipped through before selecting another, and keep only five or six books on the shelf. Of course, add books as you feel that your child is able to read them more appropriately. For those times when you are not around to supervise and you walk past the shelf to find all the books on the floor, be sure to get the child's help in placing them back on the shelf.

51 The neighbors are complaining about the noise coming from my apartment, but I have two very energetic, autistic sons. What is the best way for me to handle this situation?

As with all issues regarding getting along with others, there are some points on which you can meet your neighbors half way, and some on which you cannot. Be sure that your apartment is carpeted. Establish a fair bedtime for your children, and when they are up at night be strict about the noise they make. Make sure that their day includes a lot of physical activity so that they are tired out by the evening. In nice weather, take them out to the park or to play sports after school. In the winter, try to take them to a gym or designate running and jumping time to a specific location in the apartment at the same time each day, and join in with them. Have pillow fights, throw a soft ball back and forth, or roll around on the floor together to music. In other words, spend some time every day engaging the boys in appropriate physical activity that is not as noisy and still as energetic.

By six or seven o'clock, depending on their ages, you should be able to round your children up for a bath or a shower, serve them dinner, and sit them in front of a video before bedtime. In the morning, practice playing a tiptoe game, take turns whispering and talking – the variety of going back and forth from one to the other will make it fun, and perhaps try engaging them in a race car or dinosaur game. If they are working on a picture schedule for appropriate play, this would be a great time to take it out and practice it (for information on picture schedules, see Question 46). You can also think of other ways to make noisy play more quiet, such as playing the drums on a cardboard box.

Once you have established this kind of routine, one that is both productive to your schedule and sensitive to the neighbors around you, you can continue to live without taking their complaints too much to heart. Your neighbors know that they live in an apartment building, and that means that they will never have silence around them but rather will have to get used to the sounds of those living around them. Boys are noisy. Children are noisy. You have dedicated so much of yourself to your children and to helping them better their quality of life that you need not have to explain away the noise and the details of your daily efforts together to anyone. If you decide that you want to, have a brief conversation with your neighbors letting them know that you are doing your best, the apartment is carpeted, and that you cannot live with constant complaints either.

52   We have a four-bedroom house with a nice den and playroom, yet my son refuses to leave my side, opting to sit on the kitchen floor if I am cooking or run around the table if I am sitting at it paying bills. I would love for him to make use of the other rooms in the house and play, even if I am not sitting by his side. What should I do?

Begin by walking out of the room during activities that are so reinforcing to your child that he will not want to follow. Put in his favorite video, one that he seldom gets to see (perhaps a favorite video that you save and use solely for this occasion) and sit as far away from him as possible. As he gets more and more engrossed in the show, step out for two or three minutes at a time. Increase the time you leave the room to ten minutes, etc. until he is able to watch the entire video solo. At this point, he will probably be able to sit alone for any show on television.

Start to ease yourself away during snack-time. Cookies may be allowed only at the table. Serve your child two chocolate chip cookies with milk, or another desirable snack, and tell him you are going to the bathroom and will give him another cookie when you get back if he waits for you nicely.

The first few times that you try this, do not really go to the bathroom. As soon as you step out of the room, come right back in so that your son does not have the time to get up. Then, slowly increase the amount of time you spend out of the room. Instead of going to the bathroom, go make a telephone call, work on the computer for a short amount of time, or prepare dinner.

During your child's playtime, hand him his picture schedule, or even a single toy that he plays with nicely, and go through the same steps described above. The more your child is engrossed in an activity, the more likely he will be to continue his activity even if you slip away for a few minutes.

Increase the amount of time that your child is alone by very small increments. Your goal is that your child remain alone happily, not that he tantrum or follow you, or you will have to start the entire process from the beginning. In order for this program to be successful, your son must be able to succeed at it every step of the way.

53 My son goes from room to room gathering up all of his toys and carrying them around the house with him. He needs to take approximately ten of his small belongings with him wherever we go. How can I convince him to leave some of his things behind?

Rather than trying to convince your child to leave some of his things behind, make a decision as to how many items, if any, you deem appropriate and want to allow your child to carry.

Begin by making a list of those things that your son favors and tends to carry around. Are they specific items that he repeatedly selects to take along with him or does he select different items each time, at random? Are they all from the same category (such as figurines or vehicles), the same color or the same texture? Are they items that provide security for him because of his affection toward them, or is it that he needs to feel that his hands and arms are full?

If it is that your son favors specific toys that provide him comfort, and these are the toys that he tends to carry with him, begin by setting a limit with regard to the number of toys he may take. If your son really tends to carry along ten items with him wherever he goes, reduce the items that he may carry to seven, then five, and then two. Be firm about the number of items, but let your son select which toys he wishes to take.

If your son does not really seem to care what he is carrying, as long as his arms are full, try to come up with appropriate things for him to carry. If you are shopping, let him carry some groceries. If you are going to the beach, have him carry the towels. Make sure that he carries his own backpack and lunch box every day.

See if you can begin to reduce the size of the toys that your child selects. A key chain with a car on the end is easier and less conspicuous than carrying a case of race cars. If your son is, indeed, carrying by category, work on getting the category out of his hands and onto his clothing. For example, if your son carries dinosaur figurines, let him carry one figurine and two shirts with pictures of dinosaurs on them. The next day, take away the figurine and see if he will just carry the shirts. Finally, have him wear the shirt and hold/eat a lollipop. The lollipop will distract his hands from the need to hold the dinosaur for the first couple of days that he is wearing his shirt instead. Over time, you will be able to teach him to wear his dinosaur shirt only on Mondays and Thursdays.

If it is a color that your child is fixated on carrying, this sequence should be even easier to follow. Colors can be incorporated into hats, sun-glasses, notebooks, shoes and, for girls, even nail-polish.

If it is texture that your child seems to need, then try to provide plenty of texture manipulation at more appropriate times. Work and play with Play-Doh, glue, finger paint, sand paper, rubber, felt, sand, oatmeal, gravel, etc. In doing so, however, designate a table for texture play. Play with your child at this table for long periods of time. At first you may even want to allow your son unlimited access to these materials. Do not, however, allow any of the materials to leave the table.

Another approach you can take is to give your son a mini backpack. Write his name on the backpack and allow him to fill it with anything he wants, as long as the items remain in the backpack and he bears the responsibility of carrying it at all times.

54   My son is only interested in trains. How can I get him to play with any other toy or talk about any other subject?

Your son's fixation on trains is fairly common. Before you completely discourage this fixation, think of ways in which you can use it in order to teach him skills. Reading and comprehension can be motivated by using trains as the subject. Math can be taught by using small trains as manipulatives.

Use trains to work on counting. A child can learn colors by pointing or playing with the red train, the blue train, and then the green train and so forth. Compare big trains with little ones. Put a toy train on the table, under the table, and next to the table. Work on turn-taking as you and your son take turns pushing the train across the floor. Be creative in using your son's fixation to your advantage so that he can be motivated to learn all the lessons that you wish to teach.

Broaden your son's fixation by studying the history of trains and the locomotive. Teach him to read subway and railroad maps. If he is capable of it, get someone to teach him how trains are made. Broadening your son's fixation will make it a more appropriate one as well as give him knowledge that can lead to professional opportunities in the future.

Hopefully, so much appropriate involvement with trains may suffice to fill your son's needs with regard to the topic. If that is not the case, then it is necessary to curtail his involvement and fixation on trains to a level that is considered socially acceptable. Trains should not limit his ability to get involved in other activities and conversations.

Decide how often you wish to allow your son to play with his trains. For instance, you may decide to allow your son to play with his trains three times a day. Hang a chart on the wall of his room. The chart should indicate the day of the week, and next to each day have three empty boxes. Every time that your son takes out his trains, have him place a sticker in one of the boxes designated for the appropriate day of the week. Once all three boxes contain stickers, that is an indication to your son that he may not play with the trains again until the following day.

Additionally, set a timer as soon as your son begins to play with his trains. Decide ahead of time how long you think he should spend playing with his trains before he moves on to a different activity. Once the timer goes off, prompt him to put away his trains and play with something else. Although he will probably tantrum the first few times that you try this, the timer, as well as the chart, will help him to accept that the activity has come to an end, and to understand that there will be more opportunities for trains later or another day.

As for your son's conversations, he needs to learn that there are some situations in which discussing trains is not appropriate. If he talks about trains and you try to change the subject, make sure that he focuses and listens to what you are saying. Say to him: "Am I still talking about trains? No. Please try to answer my question." If he can stay off the topic of trains for a few sentences, then reward him. Slowly increase the length of conversation he must engage in before reverting to trains in order to get his reward. Also, make sure to reward him before he brings up trains again. Otherwise, you are rewarding him for talking about trains, not for refraining from doing so.

After your son is able to maintain a short conversation without talking about trains, teach him that he may only bring up the topic of trains one time per conversation. Try to keep conversations with your son short by creating breaks in the conversation every few minutes. If your son talks about trains more than once in those few minutes, suspend the conversation for a later time. This sounds harsh but it is an important lesson for your son to learn, as it will make him and his knowledge of trains more interesting to others, thus increasing his sociability.

Finally, practice sentences and topics with your son that lead into the topic of trains. Teach your son to listen for such sentences, and discuss trains only when the listener seems interested. Although he is probably unaware of the listener's interest level at this stage, you can work on this by showing your son a multitude of pictures of faces and body language. Review with him what each expression and stance means, and practice facial expressions and body language stances with each other.

Part 5

Reducing Unwanted and Self-stimulatory Behavior

Repetitive motor mannerisms that provide sensory input are often referred to as self-stimulatory behaviors. Such behaviors can include grimacing, hand-regarding, hand-flapping, tapping, spinning, rocking, eye-gazing, vocalizations, and more.

Although all of these repetitive motor mannerisms provide sensory stimulation, it is not always clear which sense is being stimulated. A child, for example, may tap his or her fingers for two reasons. He or she may like the feeling that the tapping makes on the tip of his or her fingers. He or she may also like to listen to the sound that the tapping produces.

In addition to being internally reinforcing, self-stimulatory behaviors are often maintained by external reinforcement. They may serve to encourage the attention of parents and teachers (Sofia scratches her arms so Mommy holds her hands). They may also help a child to get out of an unwanted activity (Michael starts to cry out by repeating short, loud screams and is led out of the classroom by his teacher).

This chapter contains plans for reducing numerous self-stimulatory behaviors common among children on the autism spectrum.

55. How can I stop my son from continually spinning?

56. How can I keep my daughter from constantly covering her eyes?

57. Our daughter stares into space for long periods of time. How can I increase her ability to focus?

58. My child is constantly flicking her fingers in front of her eyes and/or flapping her arms. How can I stop this inappropriate behavior?

59. The teachers at school claim that my daughter engages in finger-flicking self-stimulatory behavior a lot, but I am yet to see this behavior at home. I am very bothered by this discrepancy. How should I respond?

60. My child is obsessed with opening and closing doors and cupboards. How can I stop this odd behavior?

61. My daughter is obsessed with mirrors. She will stand in front of the mirror for hours, examining her hands, putting her face up close to the mirror, and repeatedly turning her head to the side to peek at herself out of the corner of her eye. Should I encourage or discourage her mirror-gazing?

62. My son obsessively touches shoes – his own, his friends', his teachers', and even those

belonging to strangers on the street. How can I get him to stop this odd and embarrassing behavior?

63. My daughter flicks the lights on and off in every room in the house. It is not so frequent that it interferes with her day, yet it is very odd behavior. Is there anything I can do about it?

64. My child spits. This is a very unpleasant and embarrassing habit, and people, including family members, avoid being around him because of it. What can I do?

65. I have a teenage child who bites. Sometimes he even bites himself. How can I stop him from hurting himself and others?

66. My son clenches his jaw in what looks like a grimace. In addition to being unpleasant to look at, this behavior is causing harm to his mouth and jaw. How can I help him relax his bite?

55 How can I stop my son from continually spinning?

Buy your son a wand. Parents who have a daughter can buy her a tutu. Allow your child to play wizard or ballerina many times throughout the day. This means dressing the girl in the tutu or the boy in a wizard hat and wand and allowing them to spin freely for an appropriate, designated amount of time. Then stop the behavior, remove the costume, and lead the child toward an alternate activity.

Take note of how frequently your child spins during the course of the day. He or she should play wizard/ballerina almost as frequently, at first, so that a pattern of appropriateness is established. Very quickly, however, start playing this game less and less frequently until you are down to once or twice a day. Whenever your child is not in costume, physically stop him or her from spinning as soon as you see this behavior occurring. Then lead your child toward a more appropriate activity. You can take this opportunity to read a book together, play a game, or have a snack.

Teach your child how to dance. Turn on the radio or a favorite CD and dance together as much as your time allows. When you dance, practice spinning once or twice and then moving on to a different dance move.

Try not to get frustrated with your child. Spinning is an addictive and exciting outlet for sensory stimulation. It is also the self-stimulatory behavior that is easiest to stop. So even if it takes much patience, time, and effort on your part, be consistent in your intervention, and you should see some positive results.

56   How can I keep my daughter from constantly covering her eyes?

First and foremost, speak to your child's pediatrician. Often children who cannot verbalize pain or discomfort will cover or rub the area that is causing them irritation. Rule out any infections or sensitivity to light as a cause. Also speak to your child's therapists to find out if and when this behavior is occurring at school.

Take a week or two to record the behavior. Whenever you see your child covering her eyes, write down the time of day, what occurred just before she covered her eyes, how long the behavior lasted, and what happened when the behavior stopped. During this week of gathering information, try to intervene as little as possible. The point is to learn about the behavior, and intervening can limit the information you may find out during simple observation.

Once you have a log of your daughter's behavior, take a close look at the antecedent, i.e. what occurred before the behavior began. Is there a pattern? Perhaps your daughter is covering her eyes after she gets frustrated with an activity. Perhaps she covers her eyes after she is over-stimulated. Knowing these answers can help you to prevent the problem before the behavior occurs by trying to eliminate the action that preceded it. In these cases, keeping her frustration to a minimum and trying to limit her exposure to over-stimulating activities and situations might help reduce her eye-covering behavior.

Next, take a close look at the consequences of the behavior. How long does the behavior last? What usually causes it to stop? A consequence that will end the behavior will have to be implemented consistently in order for it to be effective.

Interrupt the behavior as soon as you see it occurring. Take your child's hands away from her eyes, and give her something to hold and look at, such as a kaleidoscope. A kaleidoscope may provide the visual stimulation she is seeking in a more acceptable and appropriate form. Occupy her hands and her eyes, which are both physically involved in the action of eye-covering. Give your daughter a picture and ask her to point to the various people in it. Give her a lacing card to play with, or a doll and a comb and show her how to brush the doll's hair. Have her work on sorting or sing a song that has hand motions, such as "Itsy Bitsy Spider." Once she is engaged in an appropriate activity and her hands are no longer covering her eyes, ask her if she needs a rest. Perhaps this way she will be able to learn how to "cover her eyes" and take a break for a minute without actually covering her eyes.

57   Our daughter stares into space for long periods of time. How can I increase her ability to focus?

The less you allow your daughter to stare into space and tune out the world, the more connected she will be with her surroundings and the more time she will have to take in experiences and learn. Do not let her staring into space become more of a habit than necessary. Every time you catch her tuning out her surroundings, interrupt her staring and guide her toward an interesting activity. Do not ask her to stop staring. Such a request is useless in that it does not provide her with something better to do, and is counterproductive in that it calls attention to exactly that which you wish to stop. Rather than making her aware of her staring, provide her with something interesting to which she must give her attention.

Bring her crayons and paper. Put on music. Practice a program from school. Ask her a question from among those she can answer. Work on labeling body parts, items in the room, or things you see out the window. Include her in your activity. Set the table together or even give her a damp towel to use to dust off her toys.

Redirect your daughter as frequently and as naturally as you can. The more you are able to stop her staring and engage her in a more appropriate pastime, the more she will be able to participate in the world around her. The more natural your redirecting is, the more likely that natural stimuli will catch her attention in the future and stop her staring behavior without you needing to intervene.

However you decide to intervene each time you do catch her staring, be careful not to get into the habit of redirecting your daughter by calling her name. It would be counter-productive to train her, so to speak, to pay attention only when she is directly addressed by name, and "zone out" otherwise.

Although remaining on top of this behavior and constantly stimulating your daughter to pay attention to her surroundings may be very time consuming and tiring for you, it will provide the ultimate payoff when your daughter begins to "tune in" on her own more and more within a short period of time. Enlist as many family members, friends, and teachers as you can in your effort to keep your daughter's attention throughout the day. You will see quick rewards and find that the effort you need to expend will be reduced both quantitatively and qualitatively within just weeks.

58 My child is constantly flicking her fingers in front of her eyes and/or flapping her arms. How can I stop this inappropriate behavior?

There are actually two sensory stimulations that may be contributing to this behavior. One is the tactile stimulation of finger movement and the other is the visual stimulation of shape and shadow that finger-flicking can produce. In order to help this behavior decrease in frequency, try to provide the same stimulation in a more acceptable form.

To provide appropriate visual stimulation, buy your child a kaleidoscope. Blow bubbles and pop them together. Turn off all of the lights and shine a flashlight on the wall.

To provide appropriate stimulation of the fingers and hands, practice playing piano or a keyboard. Give your child a jump rope to spin while she jumps and teach her to play "Cat's Cradle" with string.

Interrupt self-stimulatory behavior whenever possible and redirect your child to a different, more appropriate activity. Do not directly tell your child to stop looking at her fingers or flapping her arms. As mentioned previously, calling attention to a bad habit only makes one more aware of that habit, and when your mind is on it, it is even harder to stop. In order to redirect your child, simply take her by the hand and lead her to a more appropriate activity.

Remember that you will probably not be able to eliminate the self-stimulatory behavior altogether. In fact, if you are successful at completely eliminating the behavior, be aware that a new one might surface and take its place. The goal, instead, is to limit the finger flicking and arm-flapping to appropriate places and times as much as possible.

59   The teachers at school claim that my daughter engages in finger-flicking self-stimulatory behavior a lot, but I am yet to see this behavior at home. I am very bothered by this discrepancy. How should I respond?

There are a number of possible reasons why your daughter is flicking her fingers at school and not at home. Perhaps she is feeling higher levels of stress at school than she is at home as greater demands are placed upon her. Perhaps she is not stimulated enough at school, and is engaging in finger-flicking out of boredom. Perhaps her teachers or classmates are giving her attention for this self-stimulatory behavior. Remember that even negative attention can be reinforcing and serve to increase an unwanted behavior rather than decrease it.

Discuss these possibilities with your daughter's teachers and ask them what they think is the cause. Remember that the teachers are the ones seeing this behavior and probably have the best idea as to why it is occurring.

Ask her teachers to keep a behavior log in which they record the time and duration of each instance of finger-flicking, as well as a detailed and precise description of the behavior, what event preceded the behavior, and what consequence followed it. This is especially important as you are never present to see the behavior occur. Together with your daughter's teachers, study the behavior log for any additional information it may provide.

If it becomes evident that, indeed, your daughter is feeling overwhelmed by the demands of the classroom, come up with a plan to ease her load. Ask her teachers which of her educational programs from her Individualized Education Plan can be postponed for next semester, and how they can slightly lower their expectations of her in the classroom in an attempt to reduce her level of stress.

If she is actually bored at school, talk to her teachers about adding some new programs to her Individualized Education Plan, teaching the old programs in a new way, or giving her fun things to do during slower, transition times of the day. For example, maybe she can keep a notebook to color in while waiting for lunch to be served, or be put in charge of pushing in the chairs when the children line up for gym.

Finally, if her self-stimulatory behavior is being maintained in the classroom by the extra attention that it gets, discuss with her teachers the option of ignoring the behavior. As long as her finger-flicking is not harmful to herself or to anyone else in the classroom, you should be able to convince the teachers to give this plan an honest try for at least a week. If ignoring the behavior does not make it disappear, then it is fair to say that the finger-flicking is not solely an attention-seeking behavior and so ignoring it will not suffice as a behavior plan.

As with most self-stimulatory behaviors, there is probably more than one reason that your daughter is finger-flicking, be it at home or at school. You may want to request to observe your daughter in school yourself. If you decide to do so, however, keep in mind that your presence in the classroom, in and of itself, is likely to alter your daughter's behavior in one way or another, and you may not be getting accurate information from your observation.

At this point, and due to the fact that you do not see the behavior occur, you may ask the principal to get involved. Let the teachers know that you trust and appreciate all that they are doing, but since you cannot form an opinion about a behavior that you do not see, you would like it if the principal could observe the behavior for any additional insight that she may provide. Invite the teachers to join you in meeting with the principal both before and after this observation session. Perhaps together you will be better equipped to come up with an appropriate behavior plan.

60 My child is obsessed with opening and closing doors and cupboards. How can I stop this odd behavior?

Begin by getting safety locks for the kitchen cupboards, thus minimizing the number of closets and cupboards your child has access to inside the home. Although this certainly will not solve the problem, it will both make your time in the kitchen calmer and remove much temptation from your child's path.

As with self-stimulatory behavior, the obsessive opening and closing of doors and cupboards is a behavior over which your child himself has little control. At the same time, it is a behavior with which a parent can easily and quickly become frustrated. In order to reduce this behavior try using two simultaneous approaches. When in public, firmly walk your child past every door, saying "This is not our door. No touching." As soon as you pass the door, offer your child a treat in the form of a candy, a kiss, or a sticker. Distract your child immediately by skipping together or by galloping. Understand that this is not offered as a solution but rather as an approach. The effects of the approach will take a long time to show. This is due to the fact that the reinforcement for obsessive, self-stimulatory behaviors comes from within, and there is very little that you or any teacher can do to make doors less intrinsically interesting to your child.

With this in mind, a second approach should be taken inside the home as well as in any other area that you are willing to consider a "private" domain. In this "private" domain, your goal should not be to eliminate the behavior, but rather to increase its appropriateness and reduce the number of times throughout the day that it occurs.

Practice

Lead your child through the door quickly and take him directly to a favorite activity, snack, or video. Practice doing this throughout the day. Select times to practice when you know that you will have the time and the energy to follow through. For instance, prepare a video in the family room. Walk your child through the door to that room quickly and sit him down in front of the video. He should be distracted enough to ignore the door. Set up cookies, ice-cream, or another favorite snack on the kitchen table. Walk your child through the kitchen door quickly and sit him down in front of his snack. The snack should be more reinforcing than the door. Create a "treat drawer" and allow your child one or two treats a day. The child may open the drawer and take the treat. He must then close the drawer once and step away if he wishes to enjoy the snack he selected.

Create a more appropriate outlet

In order to create a more appropriate outlet for the behavior that you are trying to reduce, buy stackable Tupperware containers and let your child open and close them as he pleases. For a girl, buy a four-tiered jewelry box with drawers that slide in and out. Toy houses, farms, and cars often have doors that can be manipulated, and games such as Cariboo and Guess Who have compartments that open and close. Play these games frequently, using the proper rules, so that your child gets to open and close the compartments but at the same time learns to wait his turn before doing so.

Use the obsessive behavior as a reinforcer

Although this idea may be controversial, allowing your child to open and close doors and cupboards as a reward for other good behavior will limit his engagement in the obsessive behavior while still allowing him the outlet he needs in a timely and more appropriate situation. It will also help him to improve in many other areas, as doors and cupboards will probably be one of the most potent reinforcers you will find.

Eliminating an obsession completely is nearly impossible and will turn your life and your child's life into one of constant frustration. Furthermore, elimination of such a self-stimulatory obsession will only "open the door" for another self-stimulation or obsession to take its place. Remember that your goal is to reduce the length and number of door slamming occurrences to more appropriate places and times.

61   My daughter is obsessed with mirrors. She will stand in front of the mirror for hours, examining her hands, putting her face up close to the mirror, and repeatedly turning her head to the side to peek at herself out of the corner of her eye. Should I encourage or discourage her mirror-gazing?

Discourage your daughter's mirror-gazing, especially if it is taking up a lot of time during which she can be learning and engaging in more appropriate behavior. Do not discourage her attempts to gain visual input. You can do this by limiting, rather than eliminating, her access to mirrors and by trying to make your daughter's mirror-gazing behavior more appropriate whenever possible.

For the sake of your daughter's development, arrange for your home to have only a few mirrors in it. Mirrors should be in the bathrooms and your bedroom, and perhaps have one large mirror elsewhere in the house. This mirror can be placed in the dining room, playroom, living room, or your daughter's bedroom, but not in all four. Having more than one large mirror in the house will be too distracting to your daughter and will inevitably limit her ability to participate in other important recreational activities.

Use the bathroom mirrors with your daughter twice a day. Teach her to brush her teeth in front of the mirror, comb her hair in front of the mirror, and gaze into the mirror after she washes her face. She may even take this opportunity to bring her face up close to the mirror. It is appropriate for your daughter to admire herself at the start and at the end of each day.

As for the large mirror, bring your child to mirror-gaze during selected times of the day. Choose activities for mirror-gazing that are either appropriate or can provide your daughter with a positive learning experience.

For example: after finger painting, count how many colors got on your hands. Name the colors. Then go see how many colors you and your daughter can find on your hands by looking at them in the mirror.

Have your daughter dress for the day in front of the mirror. If she can put on her own shoes, then have her do so in front of the mirror as well. Have her undress and put on her pajamas in front of the mirror. If she is verbal, ask her to describe the dressing process as she sees it. If she is not verbal, describe the dressing process to her, naming her body parts as she watches herself change her clothing.

Keep a costume trunk. During playtime, have your daughter dress up in various costumes and examine herself in those costumes in front of the mirror. Prompt her to change costumes frequently so as to limit the length of time spent in front of the mirror.

When you find that your daughter has wandered in front of the mirror on her own, you can either pull her away from the mirror and redirect her to a more appropriate, highly reinforcing activity and a snack, or you can decide to give her a few minutes to eye-gaze. If you decide to let her gaze, then after a few minutes practice more appropriate variations of what you see her doing. If she is gazing out of the corner of her eye, teach her how to do a pirouette, i.e. spin like a ballerina. If she is already spinning and swaying, bring in another mirror and show her how she can see her back by looking through one mirror into the other. Finally, practice placing your hands at the sides of your faces and work on looking in the mirror through "tunnel vision." Working on "tunnel vision" will help your daughter to use her eyes together to see straight ahead, a visual exercise that should help with maintaining direct eye contact as well.

Limiting the number of mirrors to which your daughter has access, while also guiding your daughter to mirrors when she can make use of them appropriately, will at least somewhat limit her need to engage in constant unguided mirror-gazing. Although I would not recommend completely discouraging all inappropriate mirror-gazing, I would recommend severely limiting this behavior. I would also try to make use of any opportunity that presents itself to teach your daughter better ways to gain the stimulation she seems to be seeking by staring in the mirror (as described above).

62   My son obsessively touches shoes – his own, his friends', his teachers', and even those belonging to strangers on the street. How can I get him to stop this odd and embarrassing behavior?

As already mentioned, obsessive self-stimulatory behavior is nearly impossible to stop. The question becomes, how can one limit it and increase its appropriateness? In this case, it may be helpful to buy the child a key chain in the shape of a shoe and allow him to carry it along with him wherever he goes. The shoe key chain will not eliminate the behavior, but it may slow it down a little.

Another way to slow down the child's shoe touching may be to increase his level of activity throughout the day, especially before outings. The assumption for this suggestion is that a child full of energy is more likely to bend constantly to touch shoes than one who has just played soccer for an hour, completed a running race, or won a dance contest. Evaluate your child's energy level as opposed to his daily level of activity. Perhaps adding swimming lessons to his week will help him get out his energy and at the same time slow down his tapping of shoes.

For a child who is highly aware of his behavior, it may help to create a contract together, allowing him taps on his own shoes, limited taps on parents' shoes, and none on strangers' shoes. If this sounds overreaching, try a contract in which a child who refrains from all tapping for two blocks either receives a reward or is then left alone for a block. Slowly increase the number of blocks that the child needs to complete tap-free before he can walk at ease and tap without any comments. Over time, you may be able to get him to a point where he can walk to a destination, for example the park, without any tapping, and then play on the swings and slide, or have a game of football (during which you may not remind him not to tap) and then walk home holding his key chain.

Again, in order for these plans to have a positive effect, it is of the utmost importance to remember to refrain from constantly pointing out the child's tapping behavior. Even if the reminder is well meant, it can quickly increase that same behavior that you are trying to stop.

63   My daughter flicks the lights on and off in every room in the house. It is not so frequent that it interferes with her day, yet it is very odd behavior. Is there anything I can do about it?

Give your daughter five jellybeans, coins, stickers, or other treats at the start of the day. Whenever your child flicks a light on or off, she must give up a jellybean/coin/sticker. Whenever she walks through a room without touching the light, she gets an additional candy/coin/sticker. Play this game for a full day or for a few hours or minutes at a time. At the end, count how many treats are in your possession and how many are in hers. She may eat her treats/use her coins or stickers.

Throughout the day, practice entering the room and avoiding the lights. Bring along reinforcers to give your daughter when she is successful. Make sure to practice both at home and in the community. Let the teachers in your daughter's school know about this behavior plan that you have instituted so that they may follow through with it in school as well. The more consistency and practice you can get the more quickly the flicking will stop.

64   My child spits. This is a very unpleasant and embarrassing habit, and people, including family members, avoid being around him because of it. What can I do?

Begin by posting a paper in every room of the house so that you can easily record every instance of spitting. Whenever your child spits, write down the time of day, what preceded the spitting, and what the consequences were for your child. For example: 2:00 P.M: I turned on the radio and the baby started to cry. Andrew spit. I yelled at him.

Bring along a small notebook wherever you go so that you will be able to record any spitting behavior that occurs outside the house as well. Once you have spent almost a week keeping a behavior log, look at all of the lists closely to see if you can detect a pattern.

If every time your child spits you find yourself yelling and the spitting only increases, perhaps the spitting behavior is being maintained by the reinforcement of the negative attention that your yelling provides. In this case, try to ignore the spitting as best as you can. At the same time, teach your child a better way of gaining your attention. Whenever your child spits, or even better, if you can catch him just before he is about to spit, prompt him to call out "Mommy" or tap you gently on the shoulder. Any behavior that will successfully and appropriately gain your attention can be substituted for the spitting over time and with practice.

If you find that your child is spitting whenever demands are placed on him that he finds difficult, try to ease his workload and teach him to request a break and/or help. Do not allow the spitting to be a distracter that gets him out of having to complete his task.

If the spitting is aggressive spitting aimed at peers during playtime, perhaps your child is trying to communicate that he wants a turn, a toy, or even to play, and does not have the verbal or social skills that he needs in order to do so. In this case, you may want to try saying simply: "No spitting," giving him a short time-out, and teaching him a better way to communicate with his friends. Work on turn-taking, pointing, and asking "Play?" or "Play with me?"

There is also a possibility that the spitting is occurring randomly, acting as an oral motor self-stimulation. In this case, you will want to try to find a different, more appropriate oral motor mannerism to fill that need. Teach your child to chew gum. Take time a few times a day to practice oral motor movements such as puckering lips and clicking the tongue against the roof of the mouth. Perhaps practicing oral motor movements at particular, set times of the day will eliminate the child's need to do so at random.

Disengage the child from spitting by implementing verbal imitations. Since the spitting is incompatible with verbal responses, it should stop naturally.

Once you can identify the cause of the spitting, as well as the consequence that is maintaining it, you will be better equipped to construct a program for its reduction.

65   I have a teenage child who bites. Sometimes he even bites himself. How can I stop him from hurting himself and others?

As I am sure you are aware, everyone who works and plays with your child should be told about this behavior and taught self-protection. Biting can be very serious, and even as your child is learning to stop this habit, those around him need to be constantly on the alert for their own protection as well as for your child's protection.

Before attempting any behavior plan for biting, or any other abusive habit, take a reasonable and safe amount of time to record precise notes of when the behavior occurs, what event preceded the behavior, and what the consequence was. This will give you a better understanding of when and why the behavior occurs.

Once these data are recorded, make sure that there is no medical condition causing the behavior. Children on the autism spectrum have extreme difficulty communicating most of their needs, and if your child is frustrated, biting may be the only way he can communicate that frustration. Take your child to the dentist to make sure that he is not experiencing pain in his mouth.

Evaluate your child's oral motor skills. Provide him with frequent snacks consisting of all textures, especially textures that need chewing, such as a hard-crusted bagel. If he has a biting fixation, these tougher foods can help to satisfy his need to bite. Perhaps you even want to provide him with a rubber ring that he can hold at all times and teach him to bite on the ring whenever the urge to bite surfaces.

Although one's instinct is to punish abusive behavior, punishment is not likely to be effective in this case. If the biting is occurring due to frustration, punishment can serve to increase the frustration and thus actually increase the behavior being punished, rather than decrease it. Furthermore, the punishment calls attention to the behavior, and even negative attention can make a habit harder to break. Distraction, however, can be very useful in habit-breaking. Distraction can include distraction to the mouth, such as frequent snacks and a lot of talking, verbal programs and oral motor exercise. If the child is biting his hands, have him do a lot of work that requires the use of his hands, such as sorting, typing, writing, etc. Again, allow him a lot of exercise and release of energy. Most importantly, structure his social time so that it is consistent yet limited to, say, 15-minute periods with a set activity and adequate supervision.

Use a timer to set periods of time during which he is to concentrate on not biting. If the timer goes off and your child did not bite, heavily reward him. Try to set the timer for two or three times in a row and then give your child "down time" in front of the television, or a bath, to keep the calm mood. Alternatively, set the timer for either right after or right before rigorous exercise such as jogging or a game of basketball.

Protective gear, though not ideal, should be used in the interim if the biting is causing serious physical harm. While using protective gear, remember that just as you wish to protect your child from self-abuse, you also want to work on eliminating his self-abusive behavior. Finally, remember to remind everyone who is with him that, if he bites them, they should stick their hand or body part further into his mouth rather than try to pull it out. Pulling out can increase the severity of the bite, while pushing further into his mouth will cause him to release the bite altogether.

If the behavior is addressed consistently at home and at school, a consistent message will be sent. And do not forget that a verbal child may be able to express, and need to discuss, the behavior with a therapist.

66   My son clenches his jaw in what looks like a grimace. In addition to being unpleasant to look at, this behavior is causing harm to his mouth and jaw. How can I help him relax his bite?

First, consult with a speech therapist for exercises that can help your son relax his jaw. Some of the things that the therapist may have him do can include opening and closing his mouth, moving his tongue gently around his teeth, pursing his lips, and smiling for a number of repeating trials.

Exercises should both work to develop the muscles in your son's face and jaw area, and be incompatible with the clenching. In other words, your son should not be able to clench his jaw while he is doing his exercises.

Clenching can sometimes be similar to a biting fixation. As with a biting fixation, try providing your son with frequent snacks consisting of a variety of textures. In this case, however, trial and error will tell you whether providing chewy textures eases the clenching or increases it.

If you feel that this is safe for your son and will not establish a new habit, have him practice biting down hard on a pencil for a few seconds. When he releases his bite, his jaw should be more relaxed. As soon as he starts to clench, have him bite on the pencil again. He should, eventually, learn from this to bite down only when the pencil is in his mouth. At this point, gradually reduce the number of times that you allow him to bite on the pencil to a minimum.

As for his facial expression during his clenching, practice alternate expressions with your son. The more time he spends smiling, even if his smile is contrived, the more likely he will be to smile on his own, and the more you are able to make him laugh, the more natural that smile may become.

Part 6

Teaching Social Skills and Encouraging Appropriate Interaction

Most, if not all, of the symptoms associated with autism spectrum disorder affect social interaction in one way or another. Children on the autism spectrum exhibit little, if any, eye contact. They often use people as tools by guiding their hands in order to retrieve an object that they desire. They are unable to read facial expressions or respond to social cues and gestures. They fail to interact and develop appropriate peer relationships, and prefer isolation and appear uninterested in other people.

Nevertheless, children on the autism spectrum can learn a variety of social skills that can help them interact appropriately with both adults and their peers. This chapter illustrates ways in which you can teach your child social skills and encourage appropriate social interactions.

67. My son, who has Asperger's syndrome, blurts out rude statements to and about strangers, such as: "How did you get so fat?" and "Look at the man with the funny nose." How can I teach him that these statements are both inappropriate and hurtful?

68. We live in an apartment building and my daughter is constantly pushing the neighbors so that she can get out of the elevator first. What can I do about this rude behavior?

69. How can I get my son to show more interest in other children?

70. How can I help my daughter acquire friends and play-dates?

71. How can I get my child to take turns?

72. My son, diagnosed with Pervasive Development Disorder, is a sore loser to the point where his siblings no longer include him when they play together. How do I teach him to lose more gracefully?

73. My daughter will be playing very nicely when all of a sudden she reaches over and bangs someone on the head. Sometimes she does this with her hand, but sometimes she has an object in her hand, such as a block, and can cause pain. She is a good girl and means no harm. In fact, she is very apologetic afterward. Her hitting

occurs so suddenly that it is very difficult to
stop. Any suggestions?

74. My daughter says "No hitting" as she hits her
sister. What are we doing wrong?

75. Although our children often play together, our
son with Asperger's syndrome seldom, if ever,
responds to his brother's feelings. How do I
stop this from putting a strain on their
relationship?

76. My child has Asperger's syndrome. At
dinnertime, he is either entirely focused on the
meal, or entirely focused on the conversation.
How can my husband and I help him learn to
strike an appropriate balance between the two?

77. How can I get my son to stop viewing us as
objects?

78. How can I get my daughter to react when we
walk into the room?

79. My daughter's teachers say that at school she
follows simple commands. Why is she not
listening to my instructions at home?

80. This question may seem trivial, but how can I
get my child to give me a hug every now and
then?

67   My son, who has Asperger's syndrome, blurts out rude statements to and about strangers, such as: "How did you get so fat?" and "Look at the man with the funny nose." How can I teach him that these statements are both inappropriate and hurtful?

Individuals with Asperger's syndrome are very literal and have trouble grasping and determining both the emotions of others and the facial expressions that depict these emotions. Indeed, an individual with Asperger's syndrome would not view the above statements as hurtful at all, but simply as interesting enquiries and facts. Friends and family can understand this and learn to accept such comments as they are meant, without insult, while your child works on trying to speak with a little more sensitivity to those emotions that he does not quite follow.

The question then becomes, what do you do when such comments and questions are aimed at strangers and individuals who are not aware that your child is not trying to hurt their feelings? And, more importantly, how do you teach your child to work on this behavior when your child cannot understand why or when he is being hurtful?

The first question is an easier one to answer. I would suggest saying to the child simply "I will talk to you about it later." This both answers the child and indicates to the stranger that you do not approve of the child's statement. At the same time, it does not force you into teaching your child a lesson in a public, awkward moment, nor does it force you into constantly having to explain yourself and your child's behavior to strangers.

As for how to teach your child to both recognize and refrain from making hurtful comments, there are a number of teaching methods you can try. In the instance of asking a stranger how she got so fat, you can take the beginning of the sentence "How did you get so…" and practice filling in words and their opposites. Teach the child which adjectives are viewed by most people as positive and complimentary and which as negative and insulting. In the instance of pointing out the stranger with the big nose, you can tell your child that from now on the family is going to practice commenting on objects such as buildings and trees but not on people. This will be an easier distinction for your child to make than to begin to understand the fine differences between acceptable and unacceptable comments.

Another method you can use is role playing. If your child, for instance, once commented that his sister's shirt was so bright that it made him need his sunglasses, you might want to have him watch you play the role of his sister, while the sister comments on your shirt, saying a similar comment in a less hurtful way, such as "Your shirt is as bright as the sun." Have both sister and brother come up with a number of ways to make the same statement and rate their "niceness," together. For varied exercises in appropriate social behavior, see *Social Stories*, by Carol Gray.

68   We live in an apartment building and my daughter is constantly pushing the neighbors so that she can get out of the elevator first. What can I do about this rude behavior?

Practice riding the elevator up and down with your child. Remind her during these practice runs that she is to be polite and let you exit the elevator first. Bring along a handful of small candies or pretzels. At each floor on which she refrains from pushing, hand her a reward and tell her how proud you are of her.

By practicing elevator manners, you are giving your daughter one opportunity after another to learn and drill appropriate behavior. You are also giving yourself an opportunity to work on this skill with her during a quiet time of day when the elevator and the building are less crowded. If you are less likely to encounter rushed neighbors, and you, yourself, are not on your way out, you will find that you will have more patience as well.

Keep some small treats in your handbag at all times and, whenever you find yourself in an elevator, remember to reinforce what you have practiced.

69   How can I get my son to show more interest in other children?

The best way to help your son show more interest in other children is to practice conversations, songs, and games that other children seem to be playing. Take some time to research what games and language other children who are the same age as (or a few years younger than) your son find "cool." You can do so by inviting some of your own friends with children over for lunch and observing how these children interact. Pay close attention to any popular phrases that they frequently use in speech, and to the games that they play together.

While your son is at school, go to a local private school and ask for a tour and perhaps request permission to observe one of the classrooms. Check out the playground, the pool, story hour at the library, and any other event or after-school activity that may give you some idea of what you can do with your child that is similar to his peer group's activities.

Perhaps you may be surprised and find an art class that your child could join. More likely, you may find that most boys like one sport or another, and either play that sport, watch it, or collect cards. If your son is of preschool age through the early grades, you may want to teach him who Spiderman is, supply him with some of the movie's paraphernalia, and begin to point out other children sporting Spiderman on their clothing or bags. This will spark an initial interest, if not in the other children, then in some things that they possess. It will also provide your son and the other children with a common interest and an opening for communication.

Make a mental note of words that frequent the vocabulary of children in the neighborhood, such as "Cool!" and "What's up?" Although this may seem trivial in the list of things that you need to teach your son, incorporating these words into his repertoire can be helpful in guiding him to tune in to the conversations of his peers.

Practice appropriate conversations and games. The more you talk to him and play with him as would a peer, the more likely he is to repeat the scenario. Then, create as many similar situations with peers as you can that reenact the conversations and games you have practiced. Here are some examples:

- Take your son to the park. Take along a blue pail and shovel and a red pail and shovel. Give him the blue set to play with, and sit next to him playing with the red set. Say "Which color do you have? I have a red pail and shovel," and so forth. For non-verbal children, point to the child's set and practice trading pails or shovels. Name the colors as you take turns.

  Once you have worked on a short script such as this one together, and your child is interacting nicely, get another child to participate. Bring along a sibling or a cousin or set up a play-date in the park.

  Play-dates in the park are always a good idea, as they create a situation in which children of many ages and on many different levels can find common ground to play together. Parks also provide children with the resources to go their separate ways yet still play together. Give your child the blue pail and shovel, and the other child the red pail and shovel. Most likely, one of the two children will start up a conversation. If not, point out the color difference, and let the children take it from there. By now, your son should be well versed in this conversation/turn taking and so will be more likely to show interest in the other child and his or her activity.

- Give your son a ball to hold. Ask him: "Do you like to play ball?" "Throw me/kick me the ball," and prompt him to respond. Next, you hold the ball, and say "Say: Do you like to play ball?" etc. Although this situation appears to be very unnatural, it will become more natural, spontaneous, and varied as it is practiced.

   Once that occurs, have some peers come over and supply the balls. If the conversation and game of catch do not begin on their own, facilitate it the first few times. Be careful, however, not to begin the conversation. Try to point out the balls, hand one to a child, be it your child or a friend, and fade yourself out of the interaction as quickly as possible. The point is to get your son to show interest in the other children on his own.

- Set up a Play-Doh station. Practice making balls out of the Play-Doh, rolling the Play-Doh, making foods and faces, shapes and colors, depending on your child's abilities and interests. Teach your child to ask you what you are making. Take three colors and give him only one, and prompt him to ask you to share one of the other colors. Tell him to say: "I like what you are making." (Having observed other children his age playing with Play-Doh will give you the ability to practice an age-appropriate script that will be interesting to his playmates, as well as appropriate). Practice this play situation many times. Only once he is proficient in it, create a Play-Doh table for him and some peers. With very little prompting, he should be able to transfer what he practiced with you and show interest in the other children and their shared activity.

Although practicing scripted play situations and setting up hobbies and interests such as baseball and Spiderman paraphernalia may seem unnatural, the more you create situations in which your child can succeed in approaching other children and the more tools and words with which you provide him for doing so, the more he will show a natural interest in his peers as well.

70   How can I help my daughter acquire friends and play-dates?

The answer to this question really depends on both the makeup of your neighborhood and your child's level of play skills and age. First, I would suggest trying to find a girl or boy who is two years younger than your child and can come with his or her parent for a play-date of about one hour. Prepare specific toys and games that your child knows and enjoys, making sure that anything that your child has difficulty sharing has been removed from the room in advance.

Conduct the first few play-dates with each new friend in your home. Your child will be more comfortable in a familiar environment, and the friend will be less protective of her space and more accepting of rules to which she is not accustomed.

Ask the friend to bring an activity that she enjoys as well, to share with your child. This can also be a snack if an appropriate activity cannot be found. Having the friend share something of hers will increase comradery throughout the hour.

Finally, lead the children toward crayons and stickers when other play activities are unsuccessful, or even for the last ten minutes of their playing together. Crayons and stickers are enjoyed by all ages and levels and the children can play with them alongside each other with limited interaction and a lot of fun.

Remember to keep the play-dates short even if they are a huge success. That will ensure that both children will be happy to repeat the day again soon. Two or three appropriate playmates are plenty if you rotate them as company, inviting one different child over each week or so.

Note that another option for increasing your child's social opportunities is to begin a free workshop for three to four children of your child's age in your home. Keep the workshop short, say 45 minutes, and run it yourself. Find interesting projects such as painting plaster, gluing sticks, baking and decorating cookies, or coloring a mural on a large canvas that you attach to a wall. Parents will be happy to drop off their children every other week to join in such activities, and you could supervise your child in a safe and fun environment in which she can interact with her peers.

71   How can I get my child to take turns?

Select a simple puzzle or toy that your child is already skilled at playing. When it is your child's turn, tap him on the shoulder or arm and say "Your turn." Your child may automatically take his turn, but if he does not, physically guide his hand toward the toy or game. When it is your turn, have him tap you and tell you "Your turn."

Practice, practice, practice. Three people playing will probably lead to the best results in this program. Some suggested games for working on turn-taking include: puzzles, blocks, Barnyard Bingo by Fisher Price Games, Candyland by Milton Bradley, and Topple by Pressman.

72   My son, diagnosed with Pervasive Development Disorder, is a sore loser to the point where his siblings no longer include him when they play together. How do I teach him to lose more gracefully?

Scripted situations with adults are always easier to handle than random ones with peers or siblings. Sit down to play two games with your child, and warn him ahead of time that you will probably win one and he will probably win the other. Before you play, ask him what he will do when he wins. Show him what you will do when you win. Perhaps you will clap your hands and shout "Hurray!" Maybe you will do a victory dance. Then ask him what he will do if he loses. Tell him what you will do when you lose. Maybe you will say "Man!" or ask to play again. You can even stomp one foot together. Practice these appropriate reactions a couple of times before you start to play.

Keep the game you play short, so that there is little time to forget the practiced reaction, and manipulate the game so that you each lose once and win once. Provide the reactions you practiced together. If your child said that he was going to do a victory dance, remind him that you want to see it. After he loses, prompt him to use the practiced response as well. It may take a few trials, but after he is successful, reward him with an activity together, such as a game of catch or an ice-cream party. These activity rewards should mimic activities that children might engage in during a play-date after the completion of a game.

Once you have scripted a variety of graceful losses to a variety of games, encourage other adults in your child's life to practice scripted losses with him as well. Finally, select a mature sibling to play with you. Tell both children that if they can act maturely toward each other, they will have an ice-cream party or a game of catch at the end.

Do not put pressure on either sibling to yield to the other, but rather teach them to work and play together by being sensitive to each other: "Jack may find it hard to lose and is learning how to do so nicely, so let's have some extra patience with him today. Steve, on the other hand, took time from his puzzle because he wants to spend time with you, so show him how you can play nicely." Working and playing together along with our strengths and weaknesses is a skill that we all need to work on, children and adults alike.

73   My daughter will be playing very nicely when all of a sudden she reaches over and bangs someone on the head. Sometimes she does this with her hand, but sometimes she has an object in her hand, such as a block, and can cause pain. She is a good girl and means no harm. In fact, she is very apologetic afterward. Her hitting occurs so suddenly that it is very difficult to stop. Any suggestions?

Although punishment is usually the least effective method of teaching (it must occur after every instance of the behavior in order for it to be successful), the behavior described in this question must be interrupted and stopped immediately and effectively. Every time your daughter hits, have her get up and sit on the side for one minute. The punishment must occur immediately following the behavior. One minute should be enough to be effective because your daughter knows that she did something wrong and wants to learn how to stop herself from hitting. Do not be angry with her. The hitting is almost an involuntary reflex, and although you are right to be upset, getting angry may only aggravate the situation.

If other children who play with her are in danger of getting hurt, you need to talk to them and to their parents about how to avoid injury. If the hitting is not that serious, perhaps planning play-dates with children a couple of years older than your daughter may ensure a more mature response to her hitting and allow you to work on this behavior with fewer social ramifications.

For your own understanding of this behavior, write down and chart every time that she hits. Indicate what preceded the behavior and what followed it. Perhaps you will find a pattern that you were not aware of. If your child is verbal, ask her why she hit and what she is feeling. It is very important for children to learn how to identify their emotions. Once your daughter learns how to identify her emotions, she can then learn to substitute a different behavior for hitting whenever she feels the emotion that accompanies the hit. Let her hit a pillow or a punching balloon, and when she does hit a friend, teach her to apologize. Finally, speak to a neurologist about involuntary, compulsive hitting for additional information, possible medication or exercises, and advice.

74   My daughter says "No hitting" as she hits her sister. What are we doing wrong?

"No hitting" seems to have become a phrase that your daughter has internalized, but instead of adhering to its meaning, she is echolating it in a self-created, appropriate situation. Although some believe that this behavior may be one step closer to comprehension, it is certainly not the result you are seeking.

In order to get your daughter to stop hitting her sister, it may be best to refrain completely from using the phrase "No hitting." Instead, whenever you see your daughter hitting, physically take her hands and give them something else to do, such as books to read, a doll and a comb, a drum and a drumstick, etc. Although she is not being rebuked or punished, she is being stopped, and that message will be clearer than one that she might echolate and role play later on.

75   Although our children often play together, our son with Asperger's syndrome seldom, if ever, responds to his brother's feelings. How do I stop this from putting a strain on their relationship?

I once worked with a child with autism who had a sister about two or three years older than she. She would sometimes watch our sessions, and she became quite friendly and open with me. One thing she said to me will always stay in my mind: "I know that my brother doesn't always know how to play nicely, and I understand that things are sometimes harder for him and everything. I just wish he would say 'I'm sorry.' Why doesn't he ever say 'I'm sorry?'"

I think that this little girl was right. If we can teach children with autism to say "I want" and "Bathroom" and "More, please" then we should also be able to teach them "I'm sorry." This does not mean that we expect them to understand the concept.

Rather, it is the beginning of an attempt to introduce the idea that when they do something upsetting to another child or adult, all our children, despite their level of social awareness and understanding, must apologize.

Whenever the brother, or any sibling, of a child on the autism spectrum has his or her feelings hurt, simply prompt the offender to apologize, as follows: "Say 'I'm sorry, Tony'" (insert the appropriate name in place of Tony). Whether or not the child is able to repeat the phrase "I'm sorry" is probably less important to the sibling than the recognition from you that he should, and the attempt on his part will be noted as well. Eventually, in fact, as the child does begin to learn how to say "I'm sorry," you may find that he is also learning to recognize, slowly perhaps, appropriate times for apologizing as well.

Since the siblings described in this question often play together, try introducing some new games that deal with feelings, such as Charades. Have one child act out a feeling, and ask the other to guess what the feeling is. First of all, you will be teaching the child on the autism spectrum not just to recognize feelings in the abstract, but to recognize them as they appear as expressions on his brother's face. Second of all, you will be giving the brother a more clear and concrete understanding of what his sibling knows and does not know about feelings. This greater understanding may make him more able to accept what appears to be a lack of sensitivity on his sibling's part.

Other games that you can teach your children to play together include the following: have the siblings take turns building towers and knocking them down; have the siblings take turns starting to draw or color a picture and having the other one finish it. By putting each sibling in the other's shoes you are not trying to teach them any major lesson, but you will probably see an increase of tolerance. If your son is placed in the role of the tower destroyer every now and then, he will probably be more tolerant of his sibling doing so to him sometimes. If your son gets to use his own creative artistry on his sibling's pictures every now and then, it may make up for some of his brother's marker-to-his-homework blunders (especially if you are also working on the words "I'm sorry").

Be creative and remember that, as impatient as you may become in these situations, both brothers are probably right. Your child on the autism spectrum does have a harder time taking into account the feelings of others, and your other child should not always have to be the bigger person and the understanding one. Let your children know that you feel this way, too, and they will be better equipped to accept these difficulties in their relationship with each other.

76   My child has Asperger's syndrome. At dinnertime, he is either entirely focused on the meal, or entirely focused on the conversation. How can my husband and I help him learn to strike an appropriate balance between the two?

Define and describe appropriate dinnertime behavior to your child before each meal. Then, introduce a timer during mealtime. Start by expecting your child to be able to both eat and converse appropriately for a very short period of time, say one minute. When the timer goes off, and the buzzer sounds, he can have a break. During this break, your child should still be sitting at the table but without any demands placed on him.

For each minute of appropriate dinnertime behavior, he should then get a one minute break. If, however, your child does not make it through the minute behaving appropriately, set the timer back to the beginning and start timing one whole minute of appropriate behavior. Note that if your child is frequently unable to complete the minute without the timer being set back, you may need to set the timer for 30 seconds, as a minute may be too long. Once your child is successful for numerous trials in a row, you can begin slowly to increase the amount of time for which the timer is set by 15 second intervals. Do not, however, increase the time of the break. For example, even when the child must behave appropriately for three minutes, keep the break to one minute.

If you find that your child can behave appropriately at the table for five minutes, start the same routine at five minutes with a five minute break, slowly increasing the timer by one minute intervals without increasing break time, etc. This method is most effective when utilized for more than one meal a day. Once the child is proficient and proud of long time periods of appropriate behavior, then the timer can be introduced into other meals. Be sure that the timer does not frustrate your child. Do so by setting the timer for short, successful trials and not for failure.

77   How can I get my son to stop viewing us as objects?

Frequently, children diagnosed with autism spectrum disorder will use people as objects in order to obtain an item they desire or to meet one of their needs. A child may take an adult or sibling's hand and lead him or her toward the door instead of asking to go out for a walk. The child may pull an adult to the kitchen in an attempt to get a snack or push an adult out of the way when walking by in the same way that you would push aside a toy or a chair that was in your path.

Treating people as objects has at least two causes. Children with autism often have difficulty connecting parts into a meaningful whole, viewing a hand for the function of holding things, a leg for standing or walking, and teeth for biting, for example, without necessarily understanding or taking in the way all of these parts connect to the human to which they are attached. That is why autistic children often have trouble categorizing. When asked to categorize, a child on the autism spectrum may place a table in the same category as a cat and a dog because they all have four legs, not realizing that two are animals and one is furniture.

Children with autism also tend to have difficulty with conventional communication. If your child cannot ask for more dessert, and cannot point to the enticing chocolate cake that is sitting on the kitchen counter, then your child will find a different way to indicate that he would like a piece. Sometimes, the child will tantrum. Often, the child will take an adult hand and guide it toward the item that he wants.

Whenever your child uses you or another family member in this way, prompt the child to request what he wants in a more acceptable way. In the example of the cake, for instance, you can tell your child to say "More cake, please" before giving him a second piece. If your child is not yet verbal, prompt him to use his communication board (to learn how to build and use a communication board, see Question 7).

Regardless of whether your child speaks or otherwise indicates his request, take this opportunity to work on pointing with your child. Pointing is an important skill and a lesson in development that should not be skipped. Even if your child is able to converse nicely, make sure that he can point to things he wants and also follow the pointing of others with his eyes. Practice pointing to things throughout the day and teach your child to follow your point with his gaze. Start by holding your finger close enough to his eyes so that he will not be able to ignore that your finger is there, and slowly move it to an item that your child desires. Point to a treat, a drink, a favorite doll or truck, or even a penny. Place the item to which you are pointing close, so as to practically guarantee that your child will be successful in following your point, and then reward him with what he sees. If you point to a chocolate bar, give him a piece of chocolate. If you point to a truck, let him play with it for a minute before you repeat the lesson. As your child becomes more successful at following your point, point to items that are further away and begin to fade the reinforcing qualities of the items to which you are pointing.

If your child is able to name, expressively or receptively, the members of your family, he may also be less likely to use you as a means to obtain a goal. Take pictures of each member of the family and practice pointing to them by name. You can name the family member and physically prompt your child to point to the person you named in the picture, or you can play the opposite. Point to a person in the picture and ask your child to tell you who you are pointing to. Do not forget to cheer him on when he answers correctly.

Once your child is skilled at naming family members, you can work on naming their body parts. Ask your child to "Point to Mommy's hand" and "Show me Daddy's leg." These exercises will help your child learn that your limbs are a part of you and your body and at the same time will provide him with a better, more effective, and more conventional way of expressing what it is that he would like you to do or get for him.

78   How can I get my daughter to react when we walk into the room?

Does your daughter react when she is addressed? When you ask her a question? When you call her name? The next step is, indeed, to teach her to react when you walk into the room.

Begin by facing her toward you right at the entrance of the room. Take a step toward her into the room while holding a favorite snack of hers. Hold the snack at eye level so that she must look at you before she receives the snack. If you would like, you can also verbally prompt her to say "Hello."

Once she has mastered saying "Hello" and acknowledging that you have entered the room while she is facing you at a close proximity, practice this skill when she is further into the room but still facing you. Vary the room that you use for this program so that she gets to practice it throughout the house. Take snacks along and practice in relatives' and friends' homes as well. Recruit other family members to practice with her so that she learns to react to a variety of people coming and going. Over time, trade the snack in for a book, toy, crayon, high-five, or hug. Your end goal is for a simple "Hello" back to be reinforcing enough for your child to continue to acknowledge that you or another individual has entered the room, but work on getting to this stage very slowly and as naturally as possible.

The next step is to work on this same skill when your child is facing away from you when you enter the room in which she is. Hearing the door open or hearing your footsteps enter the room is all the stimulus she should need to get her to respond. Be sure that for the first few trials she is right near the door again. This way, even with her back to you, she should clearly sense your presence.

In this program, all steps of the program should be practiced continually. In other words, you should still expect your daughter to say "Hello" when she is standing by the door facing you when you enter a room, even after you have reached the step for which you expect her to acknowledge your presence when she is at the far end of the room and facing in the opposite direction. As part of this program, it is also recommended that you teach your child to say "Goodbye" or wave when you exit the room.

79 My daughter's teachers say that at school she follows simple commands. Why is she not listening to my instructions at home?

Find out exactly what commands your daughter is able to follow at school. Is this a general observation on the part of her teachers or is it a specific program in her Individualized Education Plan (IEP) in which she is making great strides? If it is a program in her IEP, then her teachers should be able to look up "One Step Commands" and give you an exact list of all of the commands that your daughter can follow, including the exact wording that they use when giving her the instructions. Once you have this list, it may even be helpful to observe your child doing her "One Step Commands" program at school. Pay attention to the intonation of the teacher's voice. Perhaps your child is getting clues from intonation that you are not providing. Also see if the objects your child is asked to get in this program are always placed in one spot. Ask the teacher if this program is practiced with just her, or if other teachers in the classroom and in the school have worked on it with your daughter. It is important that your daughter be able to generalize her ability to follow commands across a variety of people and voices.

Once you have found all this out, take what you have learned and practice it at home. Repeat her "One Step Commands" program at home every day, first in order as done at school, and then randomly, being careful to use the same words that are in the program. If there are commands, or instructions, that are not on your daughter's list that you feel would be helpful for her to be able to follow, talk to her teachers about adding them to her IEP one at a time. They should be happy to accommodate, and the consistency of learning the instructions at home and at school using the same words will help your daughter's ability to follow what you ask of her.

If, on the other hand, "One Step Commands" is not a program that your daughter is currently working on at school, ask your daughter's teacher to make a list for a more detailed account of those instructions that your daughter is able to follow at school during the day. Are these instructions ones that are given directly to your daughter or to the entire class? Are they given in simple, short sentences? Do they all relate to classwork? Compare what you are asking your daughter to do and how you are asking her with the instructions that she is able to follow at school, and try to match your verbiage to the simple instructions used by her teachers. At the same time, ask your daughter's teachers to work on increasing the generalizability of your daughter's instruction-following by slowly and systematically increasing the length of the instruction and periodically changing the tone of voice and the instructor.

There is still the possibility that you and your daughter's teachers are indeed giving your daughter the same instructions in the same way, and that she is simply more compliant at school than at home. In this case, find out how the teachers follow up when a child does not listen to an instruction, and be absolutely consistent about following up in the same way at home. Within a very short period of time, this consistency in consequence will result in a consistency of behavior as well.

80   This question may seem trivial, but how can I get my child to give me a hug every now and then?

This question is not trivial. Physical affection is how we connect to one another and express feelings of love. You love your child and absolutely need a hug every now and then. Receiving a hug from your child will also encourage you and reinforce you in all of the hard work that you put into raising your child.

Children with autism often have difficulty with hugs and other physical contact because they often experience sensory overload that can make physical contact unbearable. This is why children with autism are more likely to wear the same item of clothing for many days in a row. Even the touch of the fabric against their skin can be too abrasive to tolerate, and a change in fabric requires the child with autism to adjust to yet a new texture. This is also why children with autism often avoid being touched.

The physical discomfort that children who experience sensory overload feel during physical contact can be greatly reduced if these guidelines are followed:

- At first, expose your child to hugs infrequently, slowly desensitizing him to physical touch.

- Warn him that he will be getting a hug. Unpredictable discomfort is always more difficult to tolerate than predictable discomfort.

- Keep your hug firm and short so that your touch is less abrasive to your child's sensitive skin.

Remember that your child's difficulty with hugs and other demonstrations of affection are related to his sensory sensitivities and are in no way a reflection of his inner feelings toward you as his parent.

Part 7

Encouraging Appropriate Behavior and Conduct Outside the Home

Children who are active community members are exposed to many learning opportunities and exciting experiences. Parents of children on the autism spectrum, however, often encounter many difficulties in taking their children to community events. Some of these events and activities may be optional. Others, such as haircuts, grocery shopping, and visits to the doctor, can be obligatory.

With proper preparation, patience, and emotional support, every parent of every child can experience a positive, successful outing. This chapter provides practical and specific plans for making any outing, be it optional or obligatory, a success.

81. My daughter adds items to our shopping cart, and I find myself coming home with extra items that were not on my list, such as ices, popcorn, or even toilet cleaner. What can I do to help our shopping trips run more smoothly?

82. We would love to be able to go out to dinner as a family, but my daughter with autism turns us into a spectacle at the restaurant. How can we make going out to eat pleasant again?

83. How can I get my child to cooperate at the doctor's office?

84. My child is terrified of haircuts. Is there anything I can do to reduce his anxiety?

85. We are a religious family, but I find myself unable to attend services due to my child's behavior. Is there a way for me to

accommodate both our religious needs and the needs of our child?

86. I take my son to the library for story hour, but he cannot sit in his chair for more than 30 seconds at a time without jumping up and running to the center of the room. Should I continue to take him to the library, and, if so, how can I make story hour more meaningful to him?

87. My child has trouble transitioning from activity to activity. How can I make transitions easier for him?

88. Even small deviations in routine cause my son to tantrum. What should I do to help our day run more smoothly?

89. My child wanders away from me and seems to have no concept of danger. How can I ensure his safety?

90. My child is too impatient to wait in line. I cannot take him to the bank, the library or even an amusement park without considerable difficulty. What should I do?

91. My nine-year-old daughter still carries her blankie around the neighborhood. I understand that this is not age-appropriate but cannot bring myself to simply throw it out and break her heart. How can I convince her to leave it at home?

92. My son is so set in his ways and routine that he tantrums if we veer so much as to take a new route to his grandparents' house when driving there in the car. I need to be able to take a different road sometimes, depending on traffic, and he needs to be able to deal better with variation and change in routine. How can I make this happen?

93. My child rides the school bus for approximately an hour and a half each day. How can I help make the bus ride to and from school more tolerable?

94. I feel that I am constantly making excuses for my child. Is there a way to avoid this?

95. I find it very difficult to accomplish simple household chores while I am with my autistic child. Everything seems to take much longer than it should. Will I always be behind?

81   My daughter adds items to our shopping cart, and I find myself coming home with extra items that were not on my list, such as ices, popcorn, or even toilet cleaner. What can I do to help our shopping trips run more smoothly?

The best way to avoid inappropriate behavior in the supermarket is to engage your daughter in the shopping process. Teach her to hold your hand and skip. Have her carry the tomatoes. Then have her carry the apples. Count steps together. Offer a prize for finding an item that begins with the letter "c." Sing "If You're Happy and You Know it Clap Your Hands," "Itsy Bitsy Spider," or any other songs that require hand motions. Ask her to point to a banana. Allow her to select a green or a red apple. Have her help you place your selections in the cart. More advanced children can count the items and even check them against a short list.

For one aisle in the store, preferably the same aisle each visit, allow your daughter to select one item to add to the shopping spree. Remember, this item is her choice. It is the one item per trip that you do not have to approve of in order for her to be able to take it home. The best aisle to use for this activity is, in my opinion, the cereal aisle. When you find yourself in the aisle that contains the cleaning supplies, practice skills and games such as "stop" and "go" or Simon Says, a game that requires use of your daughter's hands, thus making them unavailable for lifting items off the shelves.

Finally, when at the checkout counter, have your daughter help to place each item on the counter. Let your daughter return items that do not belong to the cart. Let her hand the money to the cashier. It is both an educational experience and a way to keep her involved appropriately and out of trouble. If necessary, at first, take a pretzel or a lollipop for her to eat while walking around the store.

82 We would love to be able to go out to dinner as a family, but my daughter with autism turns us into a spectacle at the restaurant. How can we make going out to eat pleasant again?

When you go out to eat, go out prepared. Select a child-friendly restaurant, and dine a little early. If you get to the restaurant at about four-thirty or five o'clock in the evening, you can still call your meal dinner and yet leave before the dinner crowd arrives. This will limit any spectacle that you feel might occur and also limit stimulation and noise, possibly encouraging a calmer evening for your daughter. The first few times you go out, select restaurants that include her favorite foods.

Before going to the restaurant, spend a few days talking about the outing. Take out a tea set and plastic foods and play diner. Teach her to select pretend foods from a menu. Then let her play the role of the waiter, prepare the foods, and serve them. Practice will make the actual restaurant less foreign and your daughter's behavior somewhat more predictable.

There are a number of additional preparations you may choose to incorporate into your evening, depending on your daughter's situation and personality. Try feeding her a snack before dinner. Although you may prefer that she eat her dinner first, making this exception will give her something to focus on while your family takes the time to order and will keep her less hungry (and hopefully less agitated) while she waits for her meal to arrive. Take along a book and some paper and crayons for when she finishes her meal and you have not. During the meal, choose your battles. Do not expect her to be able to behave, keep her voice down, eliminate all self-stimulatory behavior, keep her hands on her lap, use her fork, and eat all her peas. Decide ahead of time which two or three restaurant rules are most important for you to enforce, and let some other behaviors slide for the sake of an easier, more pleasant evening out. You can always resume work on perfect table manners at home.

Remember that the more comfortable you are in your preparation and decisions, the less you will feel like a spectacle and the more comfortable all of your children will feel, even in sensitive situations. Your daughter, even when she is having a difficult time in public, will enjoy the experience of going out and deserves those fun lessons as do the rest of our sometimes difficult children.

83   How can I get my child to cooperate at the doctor's office?

If possible, find your child a pediatrician who is accustomed to treating children with autism spectrum disorders. A good place to start your search is at your child's school, networking among other parents or at your local autism society.

Buy your child a doctor's kit and play doctor frequently. This way the instruments that a doctor uses and the act of undergoing a checkup become more familiar and can first be better tolerated in a familiar setting.

If possible, schedule appointments for times when the office is less busy. The doctors and nurses will have a little more time and patience for your child, and your child will have less of a wait in the office. Consider taking along a preferred toy, comfort item, and/or treat. Resist, however, the temptation to bargain with your child for good behavior. Explain that we do not love to visit the doctor, but we must do so for our health, and then get through the exam as quickly and efficiently as you can. A skilled pediatrician will be able to work with your child, so make sure your doctor is the right match for your family.

84   My child is terrified of haircuts. Is there anything I can do to reduce his anxiety?

Practice and play barber at home whenever possible. Start with a doll and pretend scissors. Model brushing the doll's hair, washing the doll's hair, and pretending to cut the doll's hair with pretend scissors.

Set up a "barber shop" in your playroom that you do not put away, and whenever you play the above game, place your child's doll in a toy car and "drive her" to the barber shop. Keep a mirror at the barber shop to "show" the doll her beautiful haircut.

Next, buy the Play-Doh barber shop set. Together, you and your child, as well as his therapist, can play and practice actually cutting the Play-Doh hair, as well as growing it back.

Finally, set up a vanity area with mirrors, brushes and scissors, a chair, and towels to play and practice getting a haircut at home. Start slowly, just brushing your child's hair for a few strokes and then switching roles, allowing your child to brush yours. Enlist your friends and relatives to play this game and practice so that your child gets used to many different individuals touching his hair and working with it. Once your child is comfortable with this step, pretend to cut his hair with the scissors held as close to the head as the child can tolerate. With increased tolerance, begin to cut one or two strands, heavily rewarding the child for each snip with a treat and then giving him a long break, such as a video or other favored activity.

If need be, the entire hair-cutting practice can be played in front of the television. When you decide to take your child for an actual haircut, ask around for a salon that has experience cutting the hair of children with autism. Keep in mind that, if need be, there are also hair stylists who will come to the home.

85 We are a religious family, but I find myself unable to attend services due to my child's behavior. Is there a way for me to accommodate both our religious needs and the needs of our child?

A religious family that is used to attending services should not have to compromise their religious practice because of a child with special needs. However, certain accommodations may need to be made. Before deciding on accommodations that are appropriate for you and your family or community remember that:

- Explanations to strangers in the community and personal discussions about your child can be kept to a minimum.

- You do not need to apologize to anyone for your child's special needs.

- There is no need whatsoever for you to feel embarrassed by your beautiful child who is learning more each and every day.

- You deserve to pray like any other family, even if it takes some extra effort and understanding. After all, is that not what we are praying for in the first place?

Now that you are ready to tackle the day, pack a bag to take along that includes snacks, a book, a quiet toy, and your child's favorite spinning/stimming object. Although I do not recommend allowing your child to engage in self-stimulating, inappropriate toy-play, it is fair to both you and your child to allow this sort of activity for short periods of time in order to accommodate and encourage quiet, appropriate public behavior during special events.

Get your spouse, sibling, or friend to help you. Take turns keeping your child occupied during the service. That will allow you some "down time" to enjoy being there without having to worry about your child.

At first, plan to attend half an hour to an hour of the service and, as you and your child get accustomed to this routine, stay for longer. Select a seat near an exit so that you can leave quickly and quietly if necessary. Always return to the service after such an exit, so that you can end the day with appropriate behavior, setting the stage for appropriate behavior for the following week. All this preparation for a short stay is worthwhile. It allows you and your child to be a part of the community and, with each short visit, you will see more tolerance for longer appropriate attendance.

86   I take my son to the library for story hour, but he cannot sit in his chair for more than 30 seconds at a time without jumping up and running to the center of the room. Should I continue to take him to the library, and, if so, how can I make story hour more meaningful to him?

How long is your child able to sit in a chair in other situations? Can he sit through dinner? Does he sit at school? If you were to read him a story at home, would he be able to sit and listen to the entire book before getting up? If the answer is no, then he might need to work on sitting in these situations before being exposed to having to sit in unfamiliar surroundings and listen to a story with much distraction and outside stimulation.

Talk to your son's teachers and find out if sitting is a program he is working on at school. Ask how the teachers encourage sitting in the classroom, and how long he is able to concentrate on one activity or lesson. Perhaps the teachers can offer some suggestions regarding increasing his concentration and ability to sit still at home as well as in other situations. Consistent expectations and teaching methods at home and at school will be very beneficial in seeing consistent behavior.

If the answer is yes and your son does sit nicely in other situations, then it may be very helpful to speak to the librarian before story hour and find out which books are going to be read. Read these books to your son once or twice before you go to the library. Get there early, so that your son has a few minutes to walk around and so that the two of you can select a seat that is conducive to his concentrating and to his getting up and leaving early if need be.

Many libraries and bookstores tend to include songs and projects in their story hour time. If one library does not work for you and your son, perhaps a different library or bookstore that caters to younger children may be more suitable.

Keep taking your child to story hour even if you cannot stay for the entire time. He will still gain a lot from the experience.

87 My child has trouble transitioning from activity to activity. How can I make transitions easier for him?

A child on the autism spectrum, who already has trouble appropriately categorizing the world, is bound to find transitions stressful. The best way to help children, and adults for that matter, with transitions is to limit the unknown as much as possible. Let the child know what to expect. Fewer unexpected events and changes will lead to lower levels of stress and anxiety.

Begin by taking a look at your family's routine and realistically decide which aspects of it can be held constant. Wake up at 7:00 A.M., bathroom, brush teeth, dress, breakfast, game, coat, bag, school bus. Home from school, snack, picture book, video, park, dinner, bath, story, bedtime. Routines that do not change, such as a bathroom or a morning routine, can be practiced and written down in a variety of ways.

Written schedules can be posted near the child's bed or in the bathroom/kitchen. Picture schedules can be posted or placed in an album so that the child can turn the page for each new activity in his schedule.

Schedules in a picture album are especially useful for those areas of life in which schedules do change, and are not as constant as one's morning routine. A child can be given a new schedule in an album every afternoon after school. Some days, this schedule may include going to the bank, picking up the laundry, and getting ice-cream. Other days it may include going to a party, picking a sibling up at ballet class, and going to the post office. Giving a child a schedule to work with, even if that schedule varies, adds a constant to an ever-changing, difficult-to-sort-out world.

More advanced and older children may be able to work with an oral schedule as well. Tell your child where you are going, using the opportunity to work on time concepts, as follows: "At two o'clock we are going to the library. After the library, we are going to buy you new shoes." Ask your child to repeat the schedule. Ask questions such as "What time are we going to the library?" "Where are we going after the library?" "Where are we going before we buy new shoes?"

Another way to ease transitions is to give a five minute warning. If your child has trouble with the warning, try introducing a timer. Before transitioning from one activity to the next, give your child the same five minute warning, but this time tell him that you are setting the timer, and when he hears the alarm go off, it is time to move on (i.e. leave the park, get out of the pool, etc.). Be prepared for a tantrum the first couple of weeks that you do this. If, however, you consistently use the timer and are strict about stopping each activity with the alarm, your child will become accustomed to this routine and transition much more easily in a very short period of time.

88   Even small deviations in routine cause my son to tantrum. What should I do to help our day run more smoothly?

Again, it is very difficult for a child with autism spectrum disorders to make sense of the world, and so, small details of one's daily routine can become essential to the autistic child's sense of order and provide an overall sense of security. Nevertheless, it is still difficult when your child needs to walk on the same side of the street every day, step on the same cracks, touch each door five times before entering a room, and so forth.

Keeping in mind that routine provides security, it is easy to understand the difficulty of breaking all routines at once. You will have more success with your child if you introduce one small deviation in routine at a time. This can be done in one of two ways.

One way is to try to keep all things constant as much as possible, ignoring your child's obsessive habitual behavior, but every day change one habit. Cross the street a different way, take the stairs instead of the elevator. Alternatively, you can keep all things constant but change the same thing every day, in different ways, for a couple of weeks. In other words, one day carry your child over the cracks, the next day help him jump over them, run across them, etc. A few weeks later, introduce a new change.

Implement changes in very small steps, making sure to distract your child immediately once a change has occurred. You can distract your son by asking him a question, offering him a treat, or pointing out something interesting to look at. If, despite the distraction, he begins to tantrum, try not to feed into his tantrum, but move along with the rest of the routine as he is accustomed to it. His tantrums should decrease both in length and severity.

Check with your pediatrician for other suggestions and/or medications if you feel so oriented. Try not to get frustrated with your child. His behavior is disruptive to you and to your day, but most likely is not within his control. When you have the time and the patience, take your son to practice deviations in routine that have proven difficult for him in the past. It is much easier to practice avoiding cracks in the street when you are not late for work or an important meeting.

89   My child wanders away from me and seems to have no concept of danger. How can I ensure his safety?

Teach your child the word "Stop!" Turn this lesson into a game. Whenever you are walking together, inside or outside the house, shout out "Stop!" At first, practice this lesson when you are physically close enough to your son to make sure that he actually stops, reinforcing him with praise as well as with a treat. Once he gets the hang of it, practice and play this game while allowing the distance between the two of you to become greater. Make sure that your son will stop at the corner before crossing the street, at the exit/gate of the park, before touching something hot, at the edge of a pool, and in a crowded mall.

Even after he is proficient at this game, continue to practice this skill so that it is maintained across people, places, and time.

Make sure that your child responds to his name by stopping, turning to look, and saying "What?" in a loud voice. If your child has difficulty with this, no matter what his age or level of functioning, make this program a priority both at home and in school. Many school programs do not include in this lesson the child answering "What?" Be strict about wanting a verbal response from your child when he is called. A non-verbal child can often be taught to respond to his name with a loud sound. The louder your child responds to someone calling his name, the easier it will be to find your child if he wanders out of sight.

Keep a current picture of all of your children with you at all times, and dress your child in bright colors when going to a crowded area or on a trip.

Show your child flashcards with pictures of policemen, firemen, family members, and strangers. For each flashcard, ask your child who is in the picture. Teach him to identify those individuals he can trust and those he cannot.

Finally, verbal children should be taught to answer the following questions correctly:

- What is your name?

- Where do you live?

- What is your phone number?

If your child is not verbal, consider giving him an ID bracelet to wear in case of emergency.

90 My child is too impatient to wait in line. I cannot take him to the bank, the library, or even an amusement park without considerable difficulty. What should I do?

Waiting in line can be practiced for short periods of time throughout the day. Enlist two other individuals to participate and hold up three candies, calling out "Who wants a candy?" and have your child and the other two candy eaters line up to receive their treats. Try to play this game three times in one hour, making sure that your child gets to stand in all three placements in line, i.e. first, second, and third. Be sure to play this game a few more times that same day, holding up different items as well, such as chips, a drink, or even a toy. As your child exhibits greater patience, have him line up for bathtime, hand washing, throwing basketball shots, or even doing a silly dance across the room. Practice waiting for longer and longer periods of time.

When you are out in the community in an actual line, be sure to bring along plenty of reinforcers and activities, such as books, juice, snacks, crayons, and stickers and paper on which to stick them. Try to schedule outings to the bank and the post office for both after and before highly reinforcing activities that allow the child to expend energy, such as the park and McDonalds. Finally, let the child know the schedule of the day in advance, either verbally or through a sequence of pictures that he can actually carry along with him and hold in his hand. As for amusement parks, most have accommodations for families of children with special needs to be allowed to move to the front of long lines.

91   My nine-year-old daughter still carries her blankie around the neighborhood. I understand that this is not age-appropriate but cannot bring myself to simply throw it out and break her heart. How can I convince her to leave it at home?

It is very easy for a professional to tell you that your daughter will benefit more from life if she does not immediately stand out as being different, and that after a few very difficult weeks she will be just fine if you take the blankie away. This said, you, as her mother, know just how emotionally in need of security she is and may not want to break her feelings of order, love, trust, and attachment in her already difficult and chaotic world. I would suggest testing the waters and giving life without her blankie a real and honest try.

Forget or lose it somewhere one day. Expect your child to get hysterical, and try to work through it. Forgetting and losing, however, are not permanent situations. When you can look yourself in the mirror and say that you honestly believe that you got through the original tantrum and it is still not beneficial to your child to continue without the blankie, do what you think is best. If you do end up magically finding the blankie, however, do not push or even ask your child about getting rid of it again for a few months. The more stress that your daughter is made to feel about possibly losing the item again, the more attached to it she will become.

Other ideas you can suggest or enforce after a few months of hiatus include: sewing a patch from the blanket onto a few items of clothing; turning the blanket into a dress for a doll and carrying around the doll; turning the blanket into a pillow and keeping it on her bed; cutting strips from it to use as belts or bows; or keeping a piece of it with your daughter, but inside her pocket at all times.

Be creative and decide whether you are going to make a few suggestions, push the issue, or leave it alone. Constant harassment, however, is a bad idea as it will only serve to aggravate the situation with stress and a stronger need for reassurance on the part of your daughter.

92 My son is so set in his ways and routine that he tantrums if we veer so much as to take a new route to his grandparents' house when driving there in the car. I need to be able to take a different road sometimes, depending on traffic, and he needs to be able to deal better with variation and change in routine. How can I make this happen?

Select one change to work on at a time. Plan for the change in routine. This will allow you to practice variation at a time and in a place where you will be able to be systematic in the variations to which you expose your child and stay calm through your child's subsequent meltdowns. For instance, if your child has created a routine in which he needs always to be the one to press the elevator button, enter the elevator first and stand in the far right corner for the ride, start by pushing the button yourself but allow him to continue with the rest of his routine. Find time three times a week or more to leave the house simply in order to practice this variation in routine. Press the elevator button instead of your child, ride the elevator down and then up again. Go for a short walk or practice on the way home from school. Do not practice this change in routine on the way to school or when you are feeling rushed and pressed for time.

If, as in this case, you want to work on your child being able to tolerate taking different routes to familiar destinations, such as Grandma's house, schedule a visit to Grandma with the sole purpose of taking a new route in order to get there. Although your child's meltdown may be the same, knowing that this is the purpose of your trip will provide you with greater patience for the task ahead.

Start small. Do not take a new highway, but rather drive down a different street for the length of a block or two. Then continue to use the familiar route for the rest of the way. Repeat this for a visit or two, each time veering down a few unfamiliar blocks only once during the trip, preferably close to Grandma's house in order to limit the child's anxiety and reinforce him quickly by arriving at Grandma's soon after the change in routine.

Over time, increase the amount of time during which you veer off of the familiar road, and try doing so earlier and earlier into the ride. Remember to make the change a systematic one for you but be careful not to be so systematic that your child can predict the roads that you are going to take and when you are going to take them, or he will not really learn to deal with the lack of predictability of real traffic.

93   My child rides the school bus for approximately an hour and a half each day. How can I help make the bus ride to and from school more tolerable?

Before deciding what to do about the bus ride to and from school, I would make a point of talking to your child's bus driver as well as with his teachers in order to gather as much information as you can regarding your child's behavior and demeanor on the bus, in school once he arrives, and right before he leaves. This will help you to understand whether he is tired on the bus, bored, upset, etc., and plan accordingly.

If your child is tired, try to send him with an attachment item, such as a soft pillow or teddy bear. Make sure that this item is as age-appropriate as possible. If your child does not have a comfort item such as the ones listed above, establish one by giving him a small pillow at bedtime every night that you can also send with him on the bus. The benefits of a small pillow are that it is easy to carry, pillowcases can be changed, and it is age-appropriate through adulthood (many adults will take such pillows on long car, bus, or airplane rides).

If your child is showing signs of boredom on the bus, prepare a folder for him to take along every day labeled "Bus Activities." Include in the folder a coloring book with a zip-lock of four or five crayons, a book that the child selects or that you know he loves to look at/flip through independently, and a small toy cell phone, car, action figure, or dinosaur. You can teach him how to use a walkman and send him with music he enjoys or even a story on tape. Make a mix of songs and stories from tapes that he enjoys to listen to at home. Finally, create a short, small picture album of family, friends, and places he has been to and loves. This album will both make the time he has to spend on the bus go by more quickly and serve as a wonderful learning tool, occupying his mind with interesting people and events, and activating his memory.

If you discover that your child has developed an aversion to his bus ride to and/or from school, you may want to try to have a new conversation with the bus company, trying to shorten his ride. In this case, you may even be able to get the bus driver and your child's teachers to lobby for you, claiming that it makes it harder for the bus driver to do his job and that the teachers find that the ride is influencing your child's ability to perform and learn once he finally does arrive at school.

Remember, also, that in some cases we project our own feelings onto our children. Try to have a positive outlook about the long ride. Perhaps your child is, in fact, less bothered by it and will become accustomed to the relaxing down time of simply looking out the window.

94   I feel that I am constantly making excuses for my child. Is there a way to avoid this?

It is both a blessing and a hardship that children diagnosed with autism spectrum disorders do not have any physical attributes that show that they are struggling with a pervasive developmental disorder. Strangers, as well as friends and family, may therefore often hold expectations that these children are unable to meet. What should a parent of a child on the autism spectrum do when his or her child is too rambunctious in a store? Should he or she explain to everyone present that his or her child struggles with autism? Should he or she be stricter in disciplining the child? Will being stricter even serve to change the child's behavior? Should he or she leave the child at home? Or should the parent simply continue with his or her day, ignoring the hurtful looks and stares of other adults in the community?

I believe that this question is one with which all parents of all children struggle at one point or another. I believe that the answer to all of the questions listed above, as with all parents of young children, is yes. Do not be afraid to share your struggle and your child's with your peers. It will enlighten them, explain away any uncomfortable situation, and make you feel better. If your child is being too disruptive, whether or not he has a developmental disorder that makes it harder for him to behave in public, sometimes you may have to put your foot down or decide to leave him at home for certain occasions. And sometimes it is perfectly fine to think about yourself, your child and the rest of your family, and ignore the looks and comments of other nosy individuals who do not, in this case, have any idea what they are talking about.

The important thing in this situation is to be confident with the decisions you make. If you feel that you are making too many excuses, understand that you are not obligated in any way to do so. Find a balance that you are comfortable with, knowing that you are a wonderful parent who is doing a great job raising a child under difficult circumstances. Sometimes this will be recognizable to all those around you, and sometimes, as with any parent, it will be less obvious, but still true.

95 I find it very difficult to accomplish simple household chores while I am with my autistic child. Everything seems to take much longer than it should. Will I always be behind?

In part, this will always be the case. Children, in general, need attention and move more slowly from one activity to the next. Children on the autism spectrum or with any other disability require even more time and care.

In order for you not to feel completely overwhelmed, however, it is important to prioritize. Make a list of everything that you wish to accomplish on one given day. Then, re-write the list in order of importance. Your list, perhaps, may look something like this:

- laundry
- shopping
- bank
- library
- cook dinner
- organize closet.

Next, number the list in the order of easiest to accomplish with your child to hardest to accomplish with your child. For instance, your child may be able to tolerate the supermarket, but consistently falls apart in the laundry room. Now your list should look as follows:

- laundry (6)
- shopping (1)
- bank (5)
- library (3)
- cook dinner (2)
- organize closet (4)

Look at your list. The first item on the list is the laundry. It is the most important to you, but the hardest to accomplish with your child. Cooking dinner, however, is relatively easy to accomplish with your child, but less important to you. Now select three things from your list. The three things that you select should include one that is top priority and one that is easier for your child. For example:

- laundry
- shopping
- organize closet.

Although this list is shorter than your original one, it is probably more realistic. In order to help you accomplish everything listed, think of three parallel activities that your child enjoys, and list them next to the chores. For example:

- laundry
- shopping
- organize closet
- eating pizza
- the park
- playing with stickers.

When your child comes home from school, spend some quality time together. Then give him a schedule of the day. This will prepare him for both the fun and the chores. Begin by organizing the closet. While you work, if you do not want to involve your son in the organizing process this time, then sit him down with stickers. Next, take him to the park. This way you are trading off between doing your work and giving him attention. On the way home from the park, stop at the supermarket. When you are ready to tackle the laundry, you can take along a pizza menu, have your son draw the pizza he wants to eat, or even have a pizza picnic while you are doing the laundry (though not every parent may want to set this precedent). Teach your son to participate in doing the laundry by transferring clothing from the washer to the dryer or by folding towels together. Eating pizza after the laundry is completed will reinforce his good behavior. It will also be helpful as "cooking dinner" is no longer on your list for the day.

The more you prioritize and focus on what it is that you wish to accomplish, the more productive you will feel. Be sure always to pair some chores that are difficult with some that cause less aggravation. Finally, when mapping out your day, reinforce the difficult chores by following them with fun activities and your day will run more smoothly.

Part 8

Conclusion

96. How can I work on new unwanted behaviors and outbursts that may arise?

97. What general learning techniques can I apply to help my child behave more appropriately?

96   How can I work on new unwanted behaviors and outbursts that may arise?

First, try to assess the reason for the outburst, as well as what may be maintaining the unwanted behavior. If the inappropriate behavior was spurred by environmental conditions, be aware of what levels of noise, stimulation, crowds, and educational and social demands your child can tolerate. Try to avoid situations in which over-stimulation may cause an outburst. At the same time, work on coping skills. Give your child ample warning that he will be in a crowd and practice the situation before you go. If, for instance, you will be attending a birthday party, spend a week before the party playing party games at home and singing "Happy Birthday to X." Change the name of the birthday boy or girl for each time you sing the song in order to assure generalization. If you are going to a family picnic, stage a few picnics on your front porch during which you periodically approach your child for a hug, kiss, or pat on the head and tell him how much he has grown, as would the members of your family. Teach your child to ask for a break or leave the room for a minute when the demands get to be too much for him. Even non-verbal children can learn to sign the words "break," "tired," or "too much."

Self-stimulatory behaviors, or repetitive motor mannerisms should be interrupted immediately and redirected. To interrupt the behavior, gently touch the child in the least intrusive fashion possible while at the same time ensuring a successful interruption. For example, if the child is tapping, place your hand over his. If your child is rocking, gently touch his shoulder. For verbal self-stimulation, have the child repeat simple words or phrases. Ask him a question. Answering the question will inevitably interrupt the self-stimulation, as an answer and verbal stimming are incompatible and cannot be carried out at the same time.

In fact, not just for unwanted verbalizations, but whenever you interrupt a repetitive motor mannerism, you want to redirect your child to a more appropriate behavior right away. Try to think of a new behavior that is incompatible with the original, undesirable self-stimulation. For the child who is tapping, hand him paper and a crayon. For the child who is rocking, play jump rope or jog in place, march to music or dance. If a child is engaging in extraneous verbalizations, do not point it out to him and ask him to stop, but, rather, sing. If he is singing, the verbalizations will automatically stop. If, on the other hand, you point out to him that he is speaking unnecessarily and ask him/tell him to stop, you may actually increase the behavior instead, the same way a nail-biter bites more when he is more conscious of the habit and as soon as one decides to go on a diet, natural instinct leads one directly to the refrigerator. For this reason, when redirecting, try to give as little attention as possible to your child until the more appropriate behavior is established.

When a child engages in a specific, unwanted behavior for attention, the reaction of the parent should be to ignore the behavior to the extent that this is possible. The technical term for this is extinction. Note that ignoring a behavior does not mean ignoring the child. Furthermore, it is sometimes the case that ignoring the behavior completely is not possible, such as in the instance of head-banging or biting for attention. In these cases, although you must address the behavior, interrupt it and redirect with as little attention paid to the behavior as possible so that even negative attention does not become reinforcing and serve to increase the behavior you are trying to stop.

Finally, if your child is using a maladaptive behavior to try to escape a situation or avoid a difficult task, make sure that you are not setting your demands on him at a level that is too high. Once you are sure he is able to perform at the level of standards that you are setting, be strong and do not allow his behavior to get him out of having to complete his work.

Again, be aware that, more often than not, it is more than one factor that contributes to maladaptive, unwanted behaviors in a child. With this in mind, you may have to combine numerous strategies for dealing with each behavior before seeing results and improvements in that behavior.

97 What general learning techniques can I apply to help my child behave more appropriately?

When addressing your child, speak clearly and concisely. For example, do not ask your child to hurry up and get the green, no the blue coat that you think you left on the bed in his room in the morning when you got it ready for school after breakfast. Rather, say: "Please go to your bed and get your coat." This statement has fewer elements in it. It is a precise statement that will be better understood by your child and should elicit a specific, appropriate response. Such a statement is called an Sd, or a Discriminative Stimulus. Always present your Sds, or your instructions, to your child in a clear and directive voice and be careful not to ramble.

When necessary, prompt your child to behave appropriately. Do not repeat requests or threaten with punishment. Instead, if your child is not responding as he should, physically guide him to respond in the way that you would like him to. For example, prompt him to put away the plastic toy foods in his kitchen set by placing your hand over his and guiding him to do so. As you feel your child gaining control, relax your grip and allow him to continue his task independently.

Practice appropriate behavior throughout the day, and in a variety of situations. Work on creating made-up situations that will provide you with the opportunity to practice behaviors that you wish to target. For example, if your child throws things in frustration and you would like him to practice asking for help instead, then over the course of the day give him a pen to use that does not work, put his drink too far on the table for him to reach, and give him a snack in a container that is difficult to open. Watch him struggle for perhaps five to ten seconds, and then verbally prompt him to say "Help me," or "Help me, please." If you would like to have your child work on his or her waiting skills, practice by having your children line up for their snacks, for brushing their teeth, and for receiving art supplies. When your family arrives at the table, wait a few minutes before serving dinner. When your child shows signs of frustration and is not waiting nicely, practice counting to five together in the interim.

When trying to institute a new behavior and to add it to your child's repertoire, shape successive approximations of the behavior one step at a time. Do not expect your child to be able to learn how to pour his own cereal. Start by teaching him how to get his own spoon or how to pour the milk. Do not suddenly expect your child to get dressed by himself. Teach him how to put his shirt on by facing the tag toward the back, opening the shirt with his hands from the bottom, pulling the shirt over his head, putting his right arm through the sleeve hole, putting his left arm through the sleeve hole, pulling the shirt down over his stomach and, if necessary, tucking his shirt into his pants.

If you are not sure what steps are involved in learning a specific behavior that you would like to teach, carry out the behavior yourself and write down, in detail, everything that you are doing. You may be surprised at how many steps even small tasks have. For example, reading quietly involves getting a book, turning on the light, finding a seat, opening the book, turning pages, closing the book, returning the book to the bookcase, and shutting off the light. Cleaning up one's toys involves sorting, knowing where each toy belongs, moving from one toy to the next as you clean, opening and closing closet doors, placing boxes on shelves, and more. If a task or behavior is particularly complex and requires many steps along the way, reinforce your child throughout the process and not just when the task or behavior has been achieved.

Finally, reinforce all appropriate behavior sporadically throughout the day. Let your child watch a favorite television show or video after he finishes cleaning up his toys. Tickle him for telling you that he loves you. Give him a sticker for keeping his hands to himself or a candy for keeping his tongue in his mouth. If he likes puzzles, take time to do a puzzle together after you have had a successful outing to the post-office during which your son was well behaved.

When reinforcing your child, remember that an item is only a reinforcer if your child both likes and wants it. Rotate reinforcers. A variety of candies will ensure that your child does not become bored with one taste. Pairing toys and activities with smiles and praise will help your child generalize and perform for more natural reinforcement and rewards rather than just for edible treats and stickers.

In summary, speak clearly and in sentences that are short and to the point if you want to be easily understood. Prompt your child so that he or she is shown precisely what it is that you expect him or her to do. Practice, practice, practice, and work on small steps without expecting your child to succeed at all aspects of a task at once. Finally, reinforce and praise your child whenever you can for behaving in an appropriate manner.

Part 9
Resources and References

98. What resources and publications are available to use as guides in encouraging appropriate behavior in autism-spectrum children?

99. What organizations are accessible to parents and their autism-spectrum children?

100. What are some of the web-sites that may provide additional information for parents of autism-spectrum children on reducing maladaptive behaviors and encouraging more appropriate ones?

98   What resources and publications are available to use as guides in encouraging appropriate behavior in autism-spectrum children?

Articles

Arendt, R.E., MacLean, W.E. Jr., and Baumeister, A.A. (1988) 'Critique of sensory integration therapy and its application in mental retardation.' *American Journal of Mental Retardation 92*, 401–411.

Carr, E.G. and Durand, V.M. (1995) 'Reducing behavior problems through functional communication training.' *Journal of Applied Behavior Analysis 18*, 111–127.

Lovaas, O.I. and Smith, T. (1989) 'A comprehensive behavioral theory of autistic children: paradigm for research and treatment.' *Journal of Behavior Therapy and Experimental Psychiatry 20*, 17–29.

Rincover, A. (1978) 'Sensory extinction: a procedure for elimination of self-stimulatory behavior in psychotic children.' *Journal of Abnormal Child Psychology 6*, 299–301.

Journals, newsletters, and magazines

Focus on Autism and Other Developmental Disabilities
PRO-ED, Inc
8700 Shoal Creek Blvd
Austin, TX 78757
USA
Phone: 512-451-3246 or 800-897-3202
Website: www.proedinc.com

The Journal of Applied Behavior Analysis
The Society for Experimental Analysis of Behavior, Inc
Department of Human Development, University of Kansas
1000 Sunnyside Avenue
Lawrence, KS 66045-2133
USA
Phone: 785-843-0008
Email: behavior@mail.ku.edu

Journal of Autism and Developmental Disorders
Kluwer Academic/Plenum Publishers

Subscription enquiries in North, South, and Central Americas:
Kluwer Academic Publishers, Journals Department
101 Philip Drive
Assinippi Park
Norwell, MA 02061
USA
Phone: 781-871-6600
Website: www.springerlink.com

Subscriptions in all other countries:
Kluwer Academic Publishers, Journals Department Distribution Center
P.O. Box 322
3300 AH Dordrecht
The Netherlands
Phone: 31 78 6392392

The Advocate
7910 Woodmont Ave, Suite 300
Bethesda, MD 20814-3067
USA
Phone: 301-657-0881 or 800-3AUTISM
Website: www.autism-society.org

Asperger United
393 City Road
London EC1V 1NG
UK
Phone: 020-7903-3542
Website: www.nas.org.uk

Autism and Developmental Disabilities Resource Catalog
Family Resource Services, Inc
231 Columbia Road 61
P.O. Box 1146
Magnolia AR 71754
USA
Phone: 1-800-501-0139
Website: www.frs-inc.com

Autism-Asperger's Digest Magazine
721 W. Abram Street
Arlington, TX 76013
USA
Phone: 817-277-0727 or 800-489-0727
Website: www.autismdigest.com

National Autistic Society Newsletter
The National Autistic Society
393 City Road
London EC1V 1NG
UK
Website: www.nas.org.uk

The Communicator
7 Teresa Circle
Arlington, MA 02174
USA
Website: www.autcom.org

Our Voice
P.O. Box 448
Syracuse, NY 13210-0448
USA
Website: www.ani.autistics.org

Books

American Girl Library (1998) *The Care and Keeping of You: The Body Book for Girls.* Middleton, WI: Pleasant Company Publications.

Anderson, E. and Emmons, P. (1996) *Unlocking the Mysteries of Sensory Dysfunction: A Resource for Anyone who Works with, or Lives with a Child with Sensory Issues.* Arlington, TX: Future Horizons Inc.

Attwood, T. (1998) *Asperger's Syndrome: A Guide for Parents and Professionals.* London: Jessica Kingsley Publishers.

Baker, B.L., Brightman, A. J., Blacher, J.B., Heifetz, L. J. and Hinshaw, S.P. (1997) *Steps to Independence: Teaching Everyday Skills to Children with Special Needs.* 3rd edn, Baltimore, MD: Paul H. Brookes Publishing Co.

Beyer, J. and Gammeltoft, L. (1999) *Autism and Play.* London: Jessica Kingsley Publishers.

Bondy, A. and Frost, L. (1994) *The Picture Exchange Communication System.* Pyramid Educational Consultants.

Briggs, F. (1995) *Developing Personal Safety Skills in Children with Disabilities.* London: Jessica Kingsley Publishers.

Carr, E.G., Levin, L. *et al.* (1994) *Communication-based Intervention for Problem Behavior.* Baltimore, MD: Paul H. Brookes Publishing Co.

Durand, V.M. (1998) *Sleep Better! A Guide to Improving Sleep for Children with Special Needs.* Baltimore, MD: Paul H. Brookes Publishing Co.

Durand, V.M. (1990) *Severe Behavior Problems.* New York: Guilford Press.

Foxx, R. (1982) *Decreasing Behaviors of Persons with Severe Mental Retardation and Autism.* Champaign, IL: Research Press.

Foxx, R. (1982) *Increasing Behaviors of Persons with Severe Retardation and Autism.* Champaign, IL: Research Press.

Fouse, E. and Wheeler, M. (1997) *A Treasure Chest of Behavioral Strategies for Individuals with Autism.* Arlington, TX: Future Horizons Inc.

Freeman, S. and Dake, L. (1996) *Teach Me Language: A Language Manual for Children with Autism, Aspergers Syndrome and Related Disorders.* Langley, BC: SKF Books.

Gravelle, K., Castro, N. and Castro, C. (1998) *What's Going on Down There? Answers to Questions Boys Find Hard To Ask.* New York: Walker and Company.

Gray, C. (1994) *Social Stories...All New Stories: Teaching Social Skills.* Arlington, TX: Future Horizons Inc.

Gray, C. (1994) *Comic Strip Conversations.* Arlington, TX: Future Horizons Inc.

Gray, C. (1993) *The Original Social Story Book.* Arlington, TX: Future Horizons Inc.

Gutstein, S. (2001) *Autism/Aspergers; Solving the Relationship Puzzle.* Arlington, TX: Future Horizons Inc.

Gutstein, S.E and Sheely, R.K. (2002) *Relationship Development Intervention with Young Children – Social and Emotional Development Activities for Asperger Syndrome, Autism, PDD and NLD.* London: Jessica Kingsley Publishers.

Gutstein, S. and Sheely, R.K. (2002) *Relationship Development Intervention with Children, Adolescents and Adults – Social and Emotional Development Activities for Asperger Syndrome, Autism, PDD and NLD.* London: Jessica Kingsley Publishers.

Harris, S.L. and Weiss, M.J. (1998) *Right from the Start: Behavioral Intervention for Young Children with Autism.* Bethesda, MD: Woodbine House.

Jackson, L. (2002) *Freaks, Geeks and Asperger Syndrome: A User Guide to Adolescence.* London: Jessica Kingsley Publishers.

Koegel, L.K., Koegel, R.L. and Dunlap, G. (1996) *Positive Behavioral Support: Including People with Difficult Behavior in the Community.* Baltimore, MD: Paul H. Brookes Publishing Co.

Kranowitz, C. (2003) *The Out of Sync Child has Fun: Activities for Kids with Sensory Integration Dysfunction.* New York: Perigee.

Kranowitz, C. (1998) *The Out of Sync Child: Recognizing and Coping with Sensory Integration Dysfunction.* New York: Perigee.

Lowman, D.K. and Murphy, S.M. (1998) *The Educator's Guide to Feeding Children with Disabilities.* Baltimore, MD: Paul H. Brookes Publishing Co.

Maurice, C., Green, G. and Luce, S.C. (1996) *Behavioral Intervention for Young Children with Autism: A Manual for Parents and Professionals.* Austin, TX: Pro-ed.

McAffe, J. (2002) *Navigating the Social World: A Curriculum for Individuals with Asperger's Syndrome, High Functioning Autism and Related Disorders.* Arlington, TX: Future Horizons Inc.

McClannahan, L.E. and Krantz, P.J. (1999) *Activity Schedules for Children with Autism: Teaching Independent Behavior.* Bethesda, MD: Woodbine House.

Moyes, R.A. (2002) *Addressing the Challenging Behavior of Children with High-functioning Autism/Asperger Syndrome in the Classroom: A Guide for Teachers and Parents.* London: Jessica Kingsley Publishers.

Myles, B.S., Cook, K.T., Miller, N.E., Rinner, L. and Robbins, L. (2001) *Asperger Syndrome and Sensory Issues: Practical Solutions for Making Sense of the World.* Shawnee Mission, KS: Autism Asperger Publishing.

Ozonoff, S., Dawson, G. and McPartland, J. (2002) *A Parent's Guide to Asperger Syndrome and High Functioning Autism: How to Meet the Challenges and Help Your Child Thrive.* New York: Guilford Press.

Quill, K.A. (2000) *Do-Watch-Listen-Say: Social and Communication Intervention for Children with Autism.* Baltimore, MD: Paul H. Brookes Publishing Co.

Richman, S. (2001) *Raising a Child with Autism: A Guide to Applied Behavior Analysis for Parents.* London: Jessica Kingsley Publishers.

Schroeder, S.R., Oster-Granite, M.L. and Thompson, T. (2002) *Mental Retardation, Autism and Self-Injurious Behavior: Gene-brain-behavior Relationships.* Washington, DC: American Psychological Association.

Staub, D. (1998) *Delicate Threads: Friendships Between Children With and Without Special Needs in Inclusive Settings.* Bethesda, MD: Woodbine House.

Wells, R. (1998) *Max's New Suit.* New York: Penguin USA.

Wheeler, M. (1999) *Toilet Training for Individuals with Autism and Related Disorders: A Comprehensive Guide for Parents and Teachers.* Arlington, TX: Future Horizons Inc.

Wrobel, M. (2003) *Taking Care of Myself: A Hygiene, Puberty and Personal Curriculum for Young People with Autism.* Arlington, TX: Future Horizons Inc.

99   What organizations are accessible to parents and their autism-spectrum children?

Asperger's Syndrome Education Network of America Inc (ASPEN)

P.O. Box 2577
Jacksonville, Fl 32202-2577
USA
Phone: 904-745-6741

Asperger's Syndrome Support Network

P.O. Box 123
Lawnton, QLD 4501
Australia
Phone: 617-3285-7701

Autism Association of New South Wales
P.O. Box 361
Forestville, NSW 2087
Australia
Phone: 02-9452-5088

Autism Association Queensland Inc
P.O. Box 363
Sunnybank QLD 4109
Australia
Phone: 617-3273-0000

Autism Europe
Avenue E. Van Beccelaere 26b, Bte.21
B-1170 Bruxelles
Belgium
Phone: 32-0-2 675-7505

Autism Research Institute
4182 Adams Avenue
San Diego, CA, 92116
USA
Phone: 619-563-6840

Autism Society of America
7910 Woodmont Avenue Suite 650
Bethesda, MD 20814-3015
USA
Phone: 301-657-0881 or 800-3-AUTISM

Autism Society of Canada
129 Yorkville Avenue Suite 202
Toronto, Ontario M5R 1C4
Canada
Phone: 416-922-0302

Autism Victoria

P.O. Box 235
Ashburton, Victoria 3147
Australia
Phone: 03-9885-0533

Autism West Midlands

18 Highfield Road
Edgbaston
Birmingham B15 3DU
UK

COSAC (Center for Outreach Services for the Autism Community)

1450 Parkside Avenue Suite 22
Ewing, NJ 08638
USA
Phone: 609-883-5509

Irish Society for Autism

Unity Building
16/17 Lower O'Connell Street
Dublin 1
Republic of Ireland
Phone: 071-744684

The Center for Autism and Related Disorders (CARD)

Various locations throughout the United States.
Corporate Headquarters:
19019 Ventura Blvd
Tarzana, CA 91356
USA
Phone: 818-45-2345

The National Autistic Society

393 City Road
London EC1V 1NE
UK
Phone: 020-7833-2299

Sibling Information Network
Department of Educational Psychology
Box U-64 The University of Connecticut
Storrs, CT 06268
USA
Phone: 203-486-4034

100 What are some of the web-sites that may provide additional information for parents of autism-spectrum children on reducing maladaptive behaviors and encouraging more appropriate ones?

Autism Network International
www.ani.autistics.org

Asperger's Disorder Homepage
www.aspergers.com

Asperger's Syndrome Information Sources
www.btinternet.com/~black.ice/addnet/aspergers.html

Center for the Study of Autism (1)
www.autism.com

Center for the Study of Autism (2)
www.autism.org

Autism Society of Vermont
www.autism-info.org

Autism and PDD Support Network
www.autism-pdd.net/autism.htm

Autism Resources
www.autism-resources.com

Autism Society of America
www.autism-society.org

Autism Online
www.autismonline.org

CARD – The Center for Autism and Related Disorders
www.centerforautism.com

NAAR – National Alliance for Autism Research
www.naar.org

Asperger Syndrome Information and Support
www.udel.edu/bkirby/asperger

POAC – Parents of Autistic Children
www.poac.net

Sensory Resources
www.sensoryresources.com

The SPD Network
www.sinetwork.org

Community Services for Autistic Adults and Children
www.csaac.org

Families for Early Autism Treatment
www.feat.org

KidSource OnLine
www.kidsource.com/nichcy/autism.html

National Center for Learning Disabilities
www.ncld.org

National Autistic Society (Surrey Branch)
www.mugsy.org

Parent Bookstore
www.parentbookstore.com

PlaySteps
www.playsteps.com

Toy Tips
www.toytips.com